Individualized Child-Focused Curriculum

More Redleaf Books by Gaye Gronlund

Planning for Play, Observation, and Learning in Preschool and Kindergarten

Developmentally Appropriate Play: Guiding Young Children to a Higher Level

Why Children Play: A Family Companion to Developmentally Appropriate Play

Focused Observations: How to Observe Young Children for Assessment
and Curriculum Planning, 2nd edition,
with Marlyn James

Focused Portfolios: A Complete Assessment for the Young Child
with Bev Engel

Make Early Learning Standards Come Alive: Connecting Your Practice
and Curriculum to State Guidelines, 2nd edition

Early Learning Standards and Staff Development:
Best Practices in the Face of Change
with Marlyn James

Individualized Child-Focused Curriculum

A
Differentiated
Approach

Gaye Gronlund

Redleaf Press®
www.redleafpress.org
800-423-8309

Published by Redleaf Press
10 Yorkton Court
St. Paul, MN 55117
www.redleafpress.org

First edition 2016
Cover design by Erin Kirk New
Interior design by Erin Kirk New
Typeset in Sentinel and Cinta
Printed in the United States of America
23 22 21 20 19 18 17 16 1 2 3 4 5 6 7 8

Library of Congress Cataloging-in-Publication Data
Names: Gronlund, Gaye, 1952-
Title: Individualized child-focused curriculum : a differentiated approach /
   Gaye Gronlund.
Description: St. Paul, MN : Redleaf Press, 2016. | Includes bibliographical
   references and index.
Identifiers: LCCN 2015037992 | ISBN 9781605544496 (pbk.)
Subjects: LCSH: Individualized instruction. | Individualized education
   programs. | Early childhood education.
Classification: LCC LB1031 .G756 2016 | DDC 371.39/4—dc23
LC record available at http://lccn.loc.gov/2015037992

Printed on acid-free paper

To all of the teachers with whom I come in contact

through my webinars, keynotes, workshops, and ongoing consulting:

Your delight in children and your dedication truly inspire me!

Contents

Acknowledgments

Heartfelt thanks to:

Mary Beth Hilborn and Gail Holtz at Hawken School for giving me the opportunity to work with coaches and teachers exploring the process of individualizing curriculum.

All of the coaches and teachers who contributed to this book.

The families of the children with whom the coaches and teachers worked.

The staff at Redleaf Press for all you have done to support my publications over the years.

Introduction
Delighting in Each Child

"Jalynn is full of energy that is so contagious. Every day she asks if she can jump on the trampoline and stays there jumping for at least ten minutes before getting off. She is a little jumping bean!"

"Thomas announced to me, 'I am really good at climbing walls and chasing down bad guys.' He often takes on superhero roles, reciting lines and posing in character perfectly! He is a great Spider-Man and a foreboding Batman."

"Hayley spends most of her time in the play kitchen and dress-up area making meals and setting up 'parties,' then goes around the room inviting everyone. She is all-inclusive, truly a hostess with the mostest!"

"Dante is a not a talker, but more of a watcher. Yet he doesn't miss a thing. When someone is hurt or upset, he gets one of the teachers by the hand and leads her over to the crying child. Then he sits nearby watching as the child is comforted. When his friend is calm again, he smiles and pats him or her on the back gently."

Teachers of young children delight in the many differences among the children and are so fortunate to get to know each of their unique personalities. In my workshops with teachers, I often pose a question to the group: "Is your job demanding?" The answer is a strong "Yes" from everyone. Then I ask "Is your job boring?" And the answer is a resounding "No!"

I believe that is because, as early educators, we do not deal with each child in the same way. We are not factory workers placing the same widget into the same hole over and over again throughout the day. Instead, each and every day, we are dealing with little human beings who come to us with many unique traits. They each have their own

- personalities,
- strengths,
- talents,

- interests,
- learning styles,
- family backgrounds,
- cultural influences, and
- life experiences.

Trying to meet all of the children's needs can be challenging. Yet as we do so, our work becomes even more interesting. We never have time to be bored, do we? Tired, yes. Drained, sometimes. But certainly not bored.

The Pressures of Accountability

In the twenty-first century, early childhood education is in the age of accountability. More and more research shows the benefits of early intervention and early education. Politicians and policy makers are recognizing the value of investing tax dollars in preschool education and family support. More and more states provide pre-K programs, and federal support systems are in development as well. And states are working to raise the quality of child care and early education through quality-rating systems that require programs to implement clearly defined best practices.

But this public attention brings pressures to be accountable, to show how the children are benefiting from the monies that pay for the teachers, buy the materials, heat the classrooms, and provide the meals. Different groups ask early educators for reports, data, and evidence to answer different questions.

Parents and family members ask: "What is my child learning?" "How is he doing compared to other children of the same age?" "Will she be ready for kindergarten?" "How do I know if all I see is children playing at your program?" "What do you teach?"

Funders and policy makers ask: "Where is the data that shows the early childhood program is benefiting the children?" "What statistics do you have to show they are learning?" "How will you prove they are ready for kindergarten?"

Directors and administrators ask: "What curricular strategies are you using to ensure that children are learning?" "How are you assessing their progress?" "Where is your documentation that provides evidence of each child's capabilities?" "How are you preparing them for kindergarten?"

And teachers ask: "How am I supposed to do what's right for young children, as well as what's right for each individual, and still be accountable with data, reports, assessment information, and evidence?" "Can I still implement a play-based curriculum?" "Can I use observations as my assessment process, or do I have to begin testing children?" "What are the goals for each child's learning?" "How on earth do I do it all?"

Remembering to Delight in Each Child

One of the key elements in early childhood education has always been joy. Whether teachers work with infants, toddlers, or preschoolers, they find enjoyment in their work. They laugh with children at how silly it feels when a bubble pops on their nose. They smile when children proudly show them something they have accomplished or created. They respond tenderly to all-enveloping hugs. They cheer when a child tries something that had been unfamiliar and frightening to him. They listen with full, engaged attention as a child explains her thinking about the transformation of a caterpillar to a butterfly or where the sun goes at night.

I am deeply worried that early childhood educators are losing the joy in their work. They are so pressured to assess learning and justify curricular strategies that they are forgetting that their work should be filled with delight in who each child is and what each one can do. This book is my attempt to bring back the joy and delight in being a teacher in an early childhood program.

I think the way to do that is to individualize curriculum so that each child is successful in his own way. I recognize that this is not an easy task, but I truly believe it is an *essential* one. Early childhood educators cannot help each child reach his full potential by applying a one-size-fits-all solution. Instead, they must do the following:

- Recognize the unique differences of each child.
- Celebrate those differences.
- Figure out curricular strategies that build on each child's strengths.
- Provide support to each child for areas that are challenging.

Successful teaching results in successful children—children who reach their potential. And such teaching requires individualization. So how does a teacher in an early childhood program teach effectively, with positive results for each child?

Developmental Studies

This book will introduce teachers to the process of creating Developmental Studies about individual children. A Developmental Study is a collection of documentation that pulls together information about a child. The documentation processes involved are best suited for use by teachers of older toddlers, preschoolers, and kindergartners. This documentation helps teachers assess a child's development and plan curriculum that will best meet her needs. It includes a variety of formats for documenting what is learned about each child and builds over time as a teacher gets to know the child and her family. Teachers will observe the child's interactions and experiences in their program and document their observations in different ways.

The chapters of this book focus on each step in the process of creating a Developmental Study. Guidance is given for completing each piece of documentation. Throughout the book, the assumption is that teachers will complete a full Developmental Study for each child under their care. Before beginning the process, readers are encouraged to read through the chapters describing each step and then look at the practical recommendations and suggested adaptations presented in chapter 11. In this way, teachers can determine how they want to proceed with creating Developmental Studies in their early childhood programs.

These formats have been tested by early childhood educators from around the country. I will share examples from their completed Developmental Studies throughout the book, along with comments, suggestions, and recommendations about their experiences with the various documentation formats.

Chapter 1 introduces the importance of individualizing curriculum and outlines the process and philosophical foundations for creating Developmental Studies. Chapter 2 focuses on getting to know the child and introduces a format for gathering information from families as well as additional family engagement strategies. Chapter 3 explores the importance of play as a major component of early childhood curricular approaches and the many ways that effective teachers plan for high-level, productive, and engaging play experiences for children. Learning about children's interests and favorites is the focus of chapter 4. Formats for interviewing and observing children to determine their interests are introduced. Chapter 5 explores how to go about planning for play experiences based on children's interests, with emphasis on the benefits for children when teachers follow their interests and recognize their favorites. Chapter 6 introduces the basics of the observational assessment process and gives practical suggestions for documenting observations to inform planning. Chapter 7 features suggestions for organizing documented observations in a portfolio for each child full of rich and descriptive information about the child's development, growth, and progress. The importance of ongoing teacher reflection about each child is the focus of chapter 8, and a format for deep reflection is introduced. In chapter 9, planning methods based on this reflection are introduced with special attention to individualized goals. Effective strategies and formats for sharing children's learning and progress with families are explored in chapter 10. In chapter 11, practical considerations when creating Developmental Studies are be shared. And, in chapter 12, conclusions about continuing to delight in children and their accomplishments are given.

In every chapter of this book, two key points are emphasized:

1   Teaching involves being *with* the children, being present and available, being observant and responsive.
2   Documentation should not take away from teaching. Rather, it should contribute to the teaching process by helping teachers gather the information they need to better meet each child where he is and to help him to continue to grow and learn.

Terminology Choices

It is sometimes difficult to decide on the best terms to use when writing a book for the early childhood field. The term *individualization* will be used to describe teaching strategies and curricular planning that take into account each child's needs. Sometimes the term *differentiated instruction* is used to mean the same thing. When considering the loved ones of each child, the terms *families* and *family members* will be used to recognize that not all children live with their biological parents. And while some programs use the word *teachers* to describe the professionals working with the children and others call them *educators*, throughout this book the term *teacher* will be used most frequently. Hopefully, no matter what your role in your early childhood program, you will see that all of the suggestions presented in this book are meant to support you in the important work you do with young children and their families.

The Teachers and Coaches Who Contributed to This Book

A group of dedicated early childhood professionals made great contributions to this book. All of them worked with me over time and shared their documentation as they created Developmental Studies about their children. Some of these educators also served as coaches, helping colleagues use the documentation formats in this book to individualize curriculum. To all of the following, I express my deep gratitude and appreciation. Let me tell you a little bit about each one of them.

Linda Cohn
Linda teaches two-year-olds in a half-day program at Pioneer Preschool in Solon, Ohio.

Kelly Dorinsky
Kelly teaches kindergarten in a full-day program at Lakewood Catholic Academy in Lakewood, Ohio.

Jordan Foley
Jordan teaches in the threes-through-sixes classroom at the Children's Community School in Philadelphia, Pennsylvania.

Jarrod Green
Jarrod is the assistant director at the Children's Community School in Philadelphia, Pennsylvania; at the time of this work, he was also a head teacher with two- through four-year-olds.

Mark Hopkins
Mark is lead teacher in a pre-K classroom at Allemas Kids Campus in Solon, Ohio.

Peter Kaser
Pete is a prekindergarten teacher at the Wellington School in Columbus, Ohio.

Cathy Kelly
Cathy is an intervention specialist with three- to six-year-olds for the Cleveland (Ohio) Metropolitan School District at Willson School.

Sara Milbourn
Sara is a preschool teacher and grade level coordinator at Hawken School in Lyndhurst, Ohio.

Sue Mowry
Sue is a lead teacher in the four-year-old program at Pioneer Preschool in Solon, Ohio.

Kelly Pfundstein
Kelly is a lead teacher in the four-year-old program at Pioneer Preschool in Solon, Ohio.

Teresa Reid
Teresa is an early education program specialist at Starting Point, a child care resource and referral agency, in Cleveland, Ohio.

LaVonne Rice
LaVonne is the owner, lead teacher, and director of LaParaDe Early Learning Center in Euclid, Ohio.

Laura Richter
Laura is director of early childhood at the Wellington School in Columbus, Ohio.

Brett Russell
Brett teaches preschool at Hawken School in Lyndhurst, Ohio.

Danielle Vigh
Danielle was a co–teacher in a blended regular and special education pre-kindergarten classroom for three- to six-year-olds in Cleveland Heights-University Heights, Ohio.

Kristin Walters
Kristin has been a teacher of preschoolers and, most recently, of two-year-olds at Pioneer Preschool in Solon, Ohio.

1 Staying Child-Focused and Individualizing Curriculum

Every time a new child begins in an early childhood program, the teacher embarks on a journey with the child and his family. She participates with the family in the child's developmental process, in the discovery of who he is and what he will become. The teacher may influence that process, but she will not be able to mold the child into something other than who he is fundamentally. At times, she will be surprised by the ways in which the child shows his strengths, follows his interests, problem solves in the face of challenges, and builds relationships. And she will be delighted as, hopefully, she witnesses the child's growth in understanding the world around him and using his own capabilities to the fullest.

Let's Begin by Thinking about Children

Take a moment and reflect about your experience as a teacher of young children. Then write down a few thoughts in response to each of the following questions:

What delights you about the children with whom you work?
What do you find interesting about specific children?
What have you noticed about their range of abilities?
What challenges have you seen that children face (poverty, pressures to grow up too fast, media influences)?
In the time that you have worked with each child, what growth have you seen?
What do you enjoy the most about your work with young children?

Here are some responses that teachers have given to these questions. Read through them and consider how their responses compare to yours. Do you have experiences in common? Can you relate to some of their thoughts?

What delights you about the children with whom you work?
"Their curiosity and enthusiasm for learning."
"The joy they feel when the lightbulb goes on—when they figure something out or understand something better."
"Their hugs and smiles."
"How much progress they make across the year and that I get to be a part of that."

What do you find interesting about specific children?
"How different they are from one another."
"I have some who ask me the hardest questions. I wish I had all of the answers!"
"Some will be a leader on the playground and a follower in the classroom. I'm never sure where each one will shine."
"The expertise some of them develop—like the dinosaur or train experts."
"How much they all love the movie *Frozen*—both boys and girls!"
"I'm drawn to the quieter, shy ones. I want to help them know that they are special in their own way."
"Some of them really puzzle me. I want to know them better, to connect with them better."

What have you noticed about their range of abilities?
"I'm continually amazed at the broad range of capabilities in my group of children. And they are all four-year-olds turning five!"
"Sometimes it's hard to plan activities and experiences that address the many different levels of abilities. I plan something that's either boring for some or too hard for others. I'm not sure how to get it just right."
"Every year the group is different. I see strengths and weaknesses across the group and in each child's developmental profile."

What challenges have you seen that children face?
"It seems to me that children are being asked to grow up too soon, too fast. I worry about that. I feel like I have to remind families and colleagues that they are little, that we have to protect childhood for them."
"We have children with multiple home languages. They struggle (as we teachers do) in communicating with each other."
"I worry that my children are not getting much food all weekend. They sure enjoy our breakfasts on Monday mornings."
"The pressures some children face at home to learn and memorize their ABCs or whatever are not always helping them. I've seen some very anxious children who worry too much about being wrong."
"Some children really struggle with self-regulation. They seem impulsive and often need redirection and help with self-control."
"The temptation of technology is everywhere. I'm afraid it's taking away from children playing with open-ended toys or enjoying time outdoors."

In the time that you have worked with each child, what growth have you seen?
"I'm so excited when I see a child move forward in understanding or skills. I love when we have that documented in a portfolio so the family, and even the child, can see it so clearly."
"We've had some real successes with children's behavior. They've learned to calm themselves down and initiate taking a break from the group when they need to."
"Some children's expressive language has just exploded, and they are so much better able to communicate to others."
"I love collecting writing samples because you see such a change from the beginning of the year to the end."
"We have children who will engage in play experiences now for long periods of time—even up to forty-five minutes. They're building, they're creating, they're cooperating, they're problem solving. It's so cool to see."

What do you enjoy the most about your work with young children?

"I feel like I really make a difference. Maybe not with every child, but I try."

"There are some families that I have become really close with. We live in a small town and see each other at the grocery store or drugstore, or at church. It's great to have these relationships."

"I love to sing and dance with children."

"I love to play right alongside of them. Their ideas are so interesting."

"Even if I'm down, when I see the children's smiles and feel their little arms around my neck in a sloppy hug, I feel so much better. I know the work I'm doing is important."

The Importance of Early Childhood Education

Teachers of young children *do* make a difference in children's lives. And much research has shown the tremendous lifelong benefits of appropriate intervention in the early years.

> Early childhood intervention programs have been shown to yield benefits in academic achievement, behavior, educational progression and attainment, delinquency and crime, and labor market success, among other domains. . . . Well-designed early childhood interventions have been found to generate a return to society ranging from $1.80 to $17.07 for every dollar spent on the program. (RAND 2005, 1)

The benefits cited above resulted for children who participated in programs that focused on building children's developmental capabilities and engaging families in partnership to help each child be successful. The focus of early childhood education is on children's success. Great thought is given to determining the best ways to help young children grow and learn. Excellent teachers know that to help young children succeed, they must individualize their practices.

Developmentally Appropriate Practices

Best practices in early childhood education endorse a child-focused and individualized approach. They encourage joy and learning. The National Association for the Education of Young Children (NAEYC) is the internationally recognized organization that publishes recommendations for the most effective educational approaches for children from birth through third grade. Based on extensive research, these recommendations advocate for what is called "developmentally appropriate practice." For their approach to be developmentally appropriate, early childhood educators plan all that they do with children around three primary principles:

1 They provide experiences, materials, and teacher guidance and support that are appropriate to children's age and developmental status.

2 They recognize individual needs of the children and are "attuned to them as unique individuals." They make adjustments and accommodations to the experiences, materials, and teacher guidance and support they give each child.

3 They learn about the social and cultural context in which each child is being raised and incorporate what they have learned into their program. (Copple and Bredekamp 2009, xii)

In early childhood programs, a "one-size-fits-all" approach is never developmentally appropriate. None of the following are considered to be developmentally appropriate:

- planning *only* for the whole group
- *always* doing the *same* thing with each child
- having the *same expectations* for each child in a group
- addressing *all* families' questions and concerns in the *same* way

In order for an early childhood program to be considered a high quality one, its teachers must provide opportunities for *each* child to learn, grow, develop, and thrive. Children thrive when their unique needs are addressed. And children thrive when their family members are included in a true partnership with the early childhood professionals caring for them. Best practices must be individualized for both children and families.

Throughout this book, the following statements will guide all of the recommendations.

> The goal is to be child-focused, to know each child well, and to delight in each child.

> Based on that knowledge and delight, the teacher will plan individualized curriculum to help each child be successful, to be appropriately challenged, and to thrive so that all children are supported in reaching their full potential.

Why Is Individualization Important?

"Responding to each child as an individual is fundamental to developmentally appropriate practice" (Copple and Bredekamp 2009, 9). But what are some of the reasons why individualization is important? Consider the following list of factors that teachers must pay attention to as they plan for each child's success:

1 Children's development varies widely in the early years.
2 Each child has special needs, interests, talents, personality traits, and learning styles.
3 Children's life experiences vary, affecting their knowledge, skills, and abilities.
4 Each child is being raised in a social and cultural context that shapes their lives, including language, values, and expectations.

To help us see how each of these factors influences teacher decisions and planning, let's look at some teachers' descriptions of children in their classrooms.

Wide Variability of Development

As every teacher learns, there are many differences within any group of children of the same age. Children develop at different rates, and each child demonstrates strengths in some domains more than others. The developmental profile of each child is unique. Teachers must plan ways to address children's strengths and support their challenges. Here are teachers' descriptions of two children who show both their strengths and areas of challenge across different domains or areas of learning.

> Mathias is very articulate and a quick learner. He enjoys helping out in the classroom, putting toys and materials back on the shelves, setting up the tables for snacktime, wiping them, and sweeping the floors afterward. He sometimes expresses his anger quite strongly and we need to redirect him. Mathias has other days when he appears very sad and quiet. We have been working with him on expressing his feelings.

> Chloe is one of the highest-achieving students in my kindergarten class. She's a fluent reader, and I want to make sure that I'm providing opportunities to keep her engaged and challenged. Socially, she's figuring things out, not always sure how to approach other children to engage them in play or cooperation. I am giving Chloe strategies and coaching her in more successful interactions in play and work groups.

Needs, Interest, Talents, Personalities, Learning Styles

In addition to individual rates of development, each child has specific needs, interests, talents, personality traits, and learning styles. Some children may have an identified special need—a developmental delay or a disability. Every child has personality traits and preferred learning styles that need teachers' attention. Addressing these differences in children is an important aspect of individualizing curriculum because they all affect learning. Teachers observe children and reflect on each individual in order to better teach each one. This book shares many strategies to help with that process. Here are teachers' descriptions of three children addressing their unique personalities, learning styles, and interests.

> Brandon is highly curious about the world around him. He is persistent in his attempts to learn. He has that thirst to learn things. He frequently shares what he's learned outside of school, and he shows delight and pleasure in learning. That's something that is really unique about him.

> I've noticed that Erika is very sensitive. I have to be careful with how I present issues to her—say, with a friend. I have to be extra gentle. She can get upset. She's usually a cautious observer before she jumps in to do something, and if she doesn't feel comfortable, she will absolutely refuse to do it. It seems to me almost a fear of making a mistake—perfectionism.

> The children in my kindergarten have so many interests. For Jeremy, it's toy cars; for Anita, spaceships and astronauts; and for Edward, dinosaurs and insects. I know that I can engage them more fully if I include their interests in my planning.

Children's Life Experiences

Another important area of concern across the country is the wide disparity of success for children because of their life experiences. "Some have had rich learning experiences at home, in a program, or both. . . . Some have not had the kinds of stimulating or supportive environments that contribute to optimal development and learning" (Copple and Bredekamp 2009, 112). In communities of poverty, children evidence an achievement gap compared to children who are being raised in more comfortable and predictable circumstances. Individualization can be a way to address the achievement gap and the wide disparity of success for children. Here is a teacher's description of a child who faces many challenges in her life.

> She is a four-year-old with significant hearing loss and came to our special education program with no language at all. She communicated through temper tantrums. We have very limited family contact but do know that her home life is very unstable. We are trying to teach her sign language but are seeing that she has lost skills due to very poor attendance. We suspect that no one is signing with her at home. We are working with our school social worker and engaging the family as much as possible. We know they need our support.

Social and Cultural Context

Each child is raised in a social and cultural context that influences his life. The members of his immediate family may include biological parents or adoptive or foster parents. He may be living in his grandmother's home with aunts and uncles and cousins nearby. Or he may be living far away from extended family. The language of the home may be English only or may include multiple languages. And the ways that the family members embrace their heritage and celebrate their own culture will vary from home to home. Every child is deeply influenced by family values, history, language, and culture. For programs to be truly child-focused and individualized, teachers need to learn more about each child's family and consider ways to celebrate the differences among families as well as the commonalities. Here is a teacher's description of the social and cultural context of one child's family.

> Denashi's family originally came from India and now lives in our Midwestern town. They have told us that they are Hindu and vegetarian and are spiritual people who follow yoga and meditation. Denashi has shown our class some yoga exercises and sung some songs in Sanskrit. She speaks both English and her home language fluently. However, she is rather shy in class and does not always communicate with others readily.

The Teacher as Researcher

To individualize the curriculum, teachers conduct research. Every day they study the children in their care. Children are the focus. Here are some ways teachers learn more about the children:

- They observe them in multiple experiences.
- They think about and analyze what they see them do and hear them say.
- They form hypotheses and test those hypotheses by offering children different materials, experiences, and levels of support.
- They experiment with different teaching strategies and evaluate the results.
- They draw conclusions, make adaptations, implement new processes within different parameters, and observe the results.
- They reflect, question, ponder, and wonder.

> "I write observations of the children on sticky notes. And sometimes my teaching assistant contributes. We later discuss the child's strengths and next steps for our IEPs [Individualized Education Programs]. This way we can really get at who each child is—their growth, how their strengths evolve, and where they are in their development in different domains."
> —Cathy

> "As we've paid more attention to individualizing and taken more steps to conduct in-class research about the children, our eyes have been opened to student potential. We're more focused on what we have done with a child and what has worked as opposed to just throwing things out and seeing what happens. We're much more intentional." —Sue

The Value and Importance of Documentation

As teachers spend time with the children in their care, they are continually learning about them. When I was teaching children, I felt like I was running a video camera in my head all day long. And, at the end of the day, that video camera was full of scenes that I had observed, interactions that had occurred, and my impressions about the children. As I wound down after the children left for the day, I "replayed" that internal tape and reviewed in my mind what stood out, considered what I wanted to remember, and wondered about where to go next with specific children. Sometimes this carried over into conversations with colleagues or into later reflection as I went about my daily life at home. Occasionally these thoughts would even find their way into my dreams that night!

But at times the videotape in my head was overwhelming. I had taken in so much information about the children that I had trouble sorting through it. Just relying on my memory and my own internal "videotaping" was not always sufficient to help me be the best teacher I could be.

That is where documentation is helpful. Writing down what you have observed as close as possible to the time of the observation is one way to make sure nothing is lost or forgotten. Taking photographs of children in action can jog your memory at a later time. Videotaping or audiotaping with various recording devices can also be helpful. And collecting samples of children's creations or work (such as writing samples, drawings, or paintings) can also help you get to know each child better.

But how on earth can teachers document everything they experience with children? That is impossible. If teachers documented everything they observed, they would have no time left over to interact with children and their family members.

Good teaching involves being present, available, observant, and responsive. Documentation should not take away from teaching. Rather, it should contribute to the teaching process by helping teachers gather the information they need to better meet each child where she is and to help her to grow and learn.

Teachers must plan for time-efficient ways to gather information. By planning for documentation ahead of time, they will not be overwhelmed. Rather, they will gather information that helps them better teach each child. They will have a clear idea of what they want to document and when best to do so.

Developmental Studies

In this book, we are going to explore organizing documentation for each child into a Developmental Study, which

- is a way of pulling together information about a child in order to assess his development and plan curriculum that will best meet his needs;
- includes an Individual Child Information Record, observation notes, photographs, work samples (if appropriate), portfolio documentation, teacher reflections, individualized lesson plans, and Family/Teacher Summary Reports;
- is related to early learning standards or goals taken from an authentic assessment tool.

In creating a Developmental Study, teachers use a set of formats for documentation. Some of these formats come from my previous books, and some have been designed specifically for this book. The documentation processes involved are best suited for use by teachers of older toddlers, preschoolers, and kindergartners. The Developmental Study is meant to build over time, across eight to twelve months. The documentation formats guide the teacher as a researcher. The formats

- engage teachers in a process of observation, reflection, and planning for individual children and the whole group;
- pose questions for teachers to consider as they work with the children;
- invite teachers to reflect individually, with colleagues, and with the child's family members;
- provide ways for teachers to plan experiences for children and then to observe and evaluate the results of the children's engagement in those experiences;
- help teachers document children's progress related to early learning standards or goals from authentic assessment tools;
- lead teachers in the process of linking their observations to their curricular planning, thinking in terms of individual children's needs as well as those of the whole group.

> "It's good to kind of be forced to think of individual things for individual children. I feel like in my regular practice when I'm thinking of individual children, I'm thinking only from the assessment viewpoint and my curricular thinking is only for the whole group. Creating a Developmental Study for individual children is making me connect curriculum and assessment. I feel successful in creating activities that are good for many children but came through the lens of the individual child's needs." —Jarrod

Each of the remaining chapters introduces a step in the process of individualizing curriculum by creating a Developmental Study. Each chapter introduces and explains a specific documentation format. Completed examples are shown along with teacher comments about their experiences using these formats. Two complete Developmental Studies can be found in appendix A. All of the examples are offered as a reference for review. They are not meant to be duplicated. These Developmental Studies reflect the unique characteristics of the children in the teacher's care, the families of those children, and the special aspects of that teacher's program. You will create documentation that is unique to the children with whom you work and the specific aspects of your early childhood program.

Throughout the book, the assumption is that a teacher will complete a full Developmental Study for each child. Before beginning the process, readers are encouraged to read through the chapters describing each step and then look at the practical recommendations and suggested adaptations presented in chapter 11. In this way, teachers can determine how they want to proceed with creating their own Developmental Studies.

Philosophical Principles and Assumptions

In addition to the three primary principles of the NAEYC recommendations about developmentally appropriate practice (age-appropriateness, individual appropriateness, and attention to the child's social/cultural context), there are five other philosophical principles that underlie the creation of an effective Developmental Study. All five principles are also firmly grounded in the recommendations for best practices in early childhood programs. Let's consider these five principles so that you are clear on the assumptions built into this process of planning child-focused and individualized curriculum:

1   The overarching goal is to be child-focused, to know each child well, and to delight in each child. Based on that premise, teachers plan individualized curriculum to help each child to be successful, to be appropriately challenged, and to reach his or her full potential.

2   Play-based curriculum and playful learning activities are a primary focus. Teachers plan play experiences for the children and integrate learning goals taken from early learning standards and/or authentic assessment tools into children's play.

3   Assessment is authentic, based on teachers observing everyday moments and documenting in quick checklists and observation notes organized into portfolio collections for each child. It's important for teachers to continue to develop as observers and to effectively use a variety of documentation strategies that are time efficient and do not take away from their presence with the children.

4   The most significant part of the process involves teachers connecting what they learn about children through observation to individualized curriculum planning. Teachers use their observations to plan for individual children as well as for the whole group.

5   Families and teachers are partners working together for the benefit of the child. In addition to regular communication about classroom events, teachers communicate with families through conversations at an initial intake or home visit and during twice-yearly family/teacher conferences that include portfolio sharing and summary reporting.

When you look at the five principles above, I hope you are feeling validated and supported in your present practices. As I address these principles throughout the book, you may learn some new ideas for how to put them into action. While you embark on the important process of individualizing curriculum, look at each principle in depth and reflect on your own implementation. Invite your teaching colleagues and program administrator into a conversation about each principle. Similar to learning about the children through your research, you are also learning about yourself as a teacher. Self-reflection is an important part of best practices as well.

> "My coteacher and I appreciate that this work is child-focused. There are so many layers to our jobs and this is the one opportunity that we can look at the children as individuals and consider who else benefits. We feel good thinking about individuals instead of all the other administrative things we have to do." —Sara

Two of the principles listed above are especially significant to understanding the process of creating Developmental Studies:

1   Play-based curriculum and playful learning activities are the focus.
2   Assessment is authentic, based on teacher observations.

Therefore, before I address planning and individualizing play, we will lay the foundations for these two principles. Chapter 3 will guide teachers in planning for play for *all* of the children. And chapter 6 will focus on the best ways to implement observational assessment practices.

Conclusion

Individualization is an essential part of teaching young children. It is embedded in the recommendations known as developmentally appropriate practice (Copple and Bredekamp 2009). This can be a challenging task for early childhood educators. Documentation formats can help with the process of being truly child-focused and individualizing curriculum. Ultimately, teachers will find that individualizing curriculum makes their work easier and more rewarding. In chapter 2 we explore ways to get to know each child well and to begin to build a partnership with the child's family members.

> "All of this documentation has really made my work easier. Being able to look at and reflect on all of the documentation is really helping to guide instruction. We know what children are interested in—we know what the next steps should be—rather than just pulling it out of the air." —Danielle

"Completing the Developmental Studies helped me feel really connected to the students as individuals instead of just looking at our goals. This looked at their interests, who they are." —Sara

"This has been so helpful. I've really liked it. I know this is benefiting my kids. It has definitely made me more accountable, and I like to think, a better teacher." —Cathy

Getting to Know Each Child and Family

The life of a young child is grounded in his family. Whether the child is being raised by birth parents, adoptive parents, foster parents, or other relatives or guardians, his experiences are deeply shaped by the love and support he receives in his home. His development is influenced by his parents, siblings, and extended family members. And we know that some of those influences may not always be positive. That puts an even greater responsibility on early childhood educators' shoulders to provide support for children. As the child begins in an early childhood program, his life changes dramatically. There he must learn to interact with other adults as well as with children. His world shifts to include relationships beyond family, yet even as this world expands, family is always at its core.

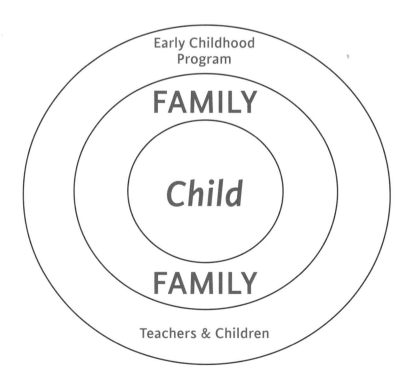

The transition from home to an early childhood program can be a daunting one for a young child. Early educators know they must create a caring, nurturing, and safe environment in which all of the children can feel comfortable as they leave behind their loved ones and the familiarity of their homes. As teachers earn the trust of children and their families, they ease the children's worries. Teachers strive to make each child feel secure enough to engage in new adventures, learning experiences, and relationships. They want each family to feel relaxed and confident that the teachers will take good care of their child. The overarching goal for early educators is to work closely with families so that each child will succeed, grow, learn, and develop to her fullest potential. This, too, is a daunting task for the educator!

So how do teachers get to know each child and family well enough to help them make a successful transition into the program? And how do they continue to learn more about each child and family so they can provide the best possible early childhood program experience for them? In this chapter, we explore ways to do just that.

Welcoming a Child and Family to the Program

Teachers know the importance of building a warm and supportive relationship with a new family as they become involved with the early childhood program. Therefore many early childhood programs conduct an initial interview or intake meeting with family members who are enrolling their child. This meeting may take place at the center or at the family's home. Or a home visit may occur after a center-based meeting to continue to build a relationship between the staff at the program and the child and his family. Open communication that is positive and friendly will begin to ease any fears or worries the family members have and make them confident that this program is the right place for their child. Teachers are earning the family's trust. They are communicating that they understand best practices for teaching young children and that they are joining them in wanting what is best for their child.

Certainly there are many important business items to include in these initial meetings, such as

- the hours the child will attend,
- the necessary medical information (vaccines and health reports),
- the appropriate group of children to which he will be assigned,
- expectations about family participation and ongoing communication,
- explanations about curriculum and teaching approaches.

Teachers will invite the child's family members to ask questions about the daily schedule, how primary caregivers are assigned, and how their child's progress will be reported. All of these items are important to include in an initial meeting with families.

It's also important to get information from them about their child. Teachers want to know more about the child's health history so they can consider the child's developmental accomplishments with this information in mind. They want to hear the family's impressions of the child's strengths, interests, and personality so they can get to know the child better. And they want to ask questions about the family's experiences as well. Are they willing to communicate more about who lives in the home or share information about their cultural heritage? Are there other important things they want the teacher to know? When teachers ask these questions respectfully and with sincere interest, they get to know families more deeply.

Perhaps the most important question to ask a family in such a conversation is this: "What delights *you* about your child?" When teachers show genuine interest in the family's thoughts and welcome their input, the child's family members feel valued and the foundation for trust is more firmly established.

The Individual Child Information Record

The Individual Child Information Record provides a format to guide these discussions with families. It includes ten conversation topics that invite family members to give their perspective about various aspects of the child's history, family situation, and development. The topics include the following:

1 The culture of the family
2 The life experiences of the child
3 The composition of the family (Who lives in the home? Are extended family nearby?)
4 The child's learning style
5 The child's developmental strengths
6 The child's interests
7 The child's emerging developmental areas
8 The child's approaches to learning and responses to challenges
9 The child's emotional makeup
10 The child's physical needs and health issues

This is the first format to complete for the Developmental Study for each child. You can find a blank copy of this format in appendix B or download a PDF version from www.redleafpress.org/Individualized-Child-Focused-Curriculum-P1426.aspx.

Individual Child Information Record

Child: _____   Date: _____

Culture	Life Experiences	Family	Learning Style	Developmental Strengths
Interests	Emerging Developmental Areas	Approaches to Learning and Responses to Challenges	Emotional Makeup	Physical Needs and Health Issues

Teachers complete this format as they meet with families either at the program or their homes. The ten categories are the focus of the conversation. Teachers take notes as they converse with the child's family members, or they complete the form after the conversation. Teachers report that these topics help them ask important questions they may not have included in formal intake meetings in the past. And family members respond positively to the teacher's interest in their child.

> "I completed the Individual Child Information Records through a conversation with each family at what I call our 'front porch visits' at their homes in August. We met for about fifteen to thirty minutes."
> —Kelly

> "I really like this format—very user friendly—great for families. And I think it will be great for transition to kindergarten, too. I talked with parents for about half an hour, and they gave me lots of information related to the form. It helped me do some goal setting right off with each family. I also revisited with the family during conferences. I definitely keep learning more about the children and can keep adding information about them." —Danielle

"Until I met with his family, I had no idea that Malik (who is four years old) had nine siblings between both parents. He has a brother who is twenty years old and a sister who is three. That gave me more perspective about Malik's family life." —Mark

Here are two examples of completed Individual Child Information Records for you to review. In addition, you will find other examples of completed ones in the full Developmental Studies in appendix A. As you review all of these completed formats, consider the following questions:

- What do you learn about each of these children?
- Do you have a beginning sense of who this child is and what his or her life experiences have been?

Individual Child Information Record

Child: Kevin   Date: September 19th

Culture	Life Experiences	Family	Learning Style	Developmental Strengths
Chinese and Korean	Active in the Chinese American community	Mom/Dad; big sister, Emily; Grandpa (whom he calls Gong-Gong); and Grandma whom he calls Paw-Paw. She speaks little English, mostly Cantonese.	Very social Likes to play	He's excited, personable, will play with anything, listens, and is curious.
Interests	Emerging Developmental Areas	Approaches to Learning and Responses to Challenges	Emotional Makeup	Physical Needs and Health Issues
Food Piano Soccer Baseball	Talks through issues Is learning to stand up for himself in play	Will ask an adult for help when needed	Good-hearted, caring	Working on potty training Separation from family members can be difficult

Individual Child Information Record

Child: Annie   Date: September 15th

Culture	Life Experiences	Family	Learning Style	Developmental Strengths
Caucasian, Midwesterners	Just moved into Dad's childhood home Family loves nature and being outdoors	Mom, Janice Dad, Carl Brother Jacob (Pre-K) Brother Cole (2 yrs. old)	Kinesthetic Visual	Very independent Recognizing and writing some letters

Interests	Emerging Developmental Areas	Approaches to Learning and Responses to Challenges	Emotional Makeup	Physical Needs and Health Issues
Gymnastics Dress up (especially *Frozen!*) Puzzles	Social growth—she prefers individual play and small groups of children Working on expressing her needs	Very independent Persistent	Mom reports that she can be "silently defiant" when she's very invested in something. Likes to snuggle and talk it out when she's upset She might not express if something is wrong—she may keep it inside.	None

The Individual Child Information Record can continue to be a helpful tool as teachers work with a child across time. They can add information in the ten categories as they get to know the child and her family better. There is no need to begin a completely new form. Instead, they add information to the original form and date their additions as they write them. They may want to consider using a different color ink to write the new items so they will easily remember which pieces of information came from the family in the original meeting and which pieces they have added and at what times.

Teachers can pull out a child's individual record occasionally, or they can be more intentional and plan to review and revise it before each time they meet with the child's family members in a formal family/teacher conference. They can also use it in the conference itself and ask the family if they have any different thoughts or perspectives related to the ten categories as they reflect about the child at this point. In this way, the Individual Child Information Record becomes a dynamic, growing document that reflects some of what the teacher and the family are learning and thinking about the child.

Here is an example of an Individual Child Information Record on which information was noted three times across a year. As you read through this example, consider the following questions:

- Are you learning more about the child with each new entry?
- Can you see this as a useful tool in your work with children?
- How often might you revisit this format to capture information that you and your colleagues are learning about children?
- How will you invite the family to give ongoing information and reflections about their child?

Individual Child Information Record

Child: Daniel   Date: 9/10/13, 11/3/13, 2/20/14

Culture	Life Experiences	Family	Learning Style	Developmental Strengths
9/10/13: African American	9/10/13: Small family Family events Holidays Going to the playground	9/10/13: Mother and father, married 2 older brothers (David, 11, and Donald, 7)	11/3/13: Observes before he jumps into a new activity Does not refuse to try if it's done during work time Catches on quickly and shares knowledge with his peers 2/20/14: Taking more risks	11/3/13: Social Creative thinking Problem solving Self-management 2/20/14: Rhyming Creativity Self-management

Interests	Emerging Developmental Areas	Approaches to Learning and Responses to Challenges	Emotional Makeup	Physical Needs and Health Issues
11/3/13: Cars Restaurant Cooking Block building Board games 2/20/14: Playing family Playing with doll house Baking using playdough in art area	11/3/13: Number knowledge Letter knowledge Shapes 2/20/14: Identifying words with the same initial and final sounds	11/3/13: Observer Persistent Focused 2/20/14: Risk-taker Patient	11/3/13: Focused and can ignore behaviors during circle, story and small-group work time Resilient	9/10/13: None

Additional Ideas for Getting to Know Families

As we move forward in this book, other formats for documenting information about the children will be introduced. Each child's Developmental Study will become a rich source of information about him and his experience at the program. Teachers will continue to interact with the child's family members about different pieces of documentation, sharing with them the many things they are learning about their child.

There are additional ideas for teachers to consider as they encourage families to participate in the program and continue to build strong, positive relationships with them. Teachers work to invite more reciprocal communication with families about their children's learning, growth, and development. Look at this list of ideas for getting to know families. Which ones do you already do at your program? Which ones are new to you? What can you do to implement some of the new possibilities presented here? What other ideas do you and your colleagues have for getting to know families well?

- Open-door policy—welcoming families (parents, siblings, extended family) to drop in at any time
- Stay and play—encouraging family members to stay after drop-off or come before pickup to play or read books with children
- Volunteer—inviting them to volunteer to help with activities (such as art projects or cooking)
- Family of the week—having a "family of the week" where each family takes turns sharing information about themselves with the children
- Special events—hosting families for potluck dinners, discussion groups, playdates, or more focused activities such as a literacy event, a family/child cooking experience, a family get-together at a local park, or a multicultural celebration

Conclusion

Early educators and families are in partnership, working together to support children. Teachers and family members are on the same team—the child's team! When teachers welcome families and provide multiple opportunities for them to participate in their program, they are building a sense of trust. As teachers get to know families, as families gain confidence in the teachers' commitment to their children, and as they get to know each other, the program will be seen as a warm and friendly place for all. Children will sense the warm, friendly atmosphere and will relax and truly be themselves when they know that all of the adults involved are working together to help them grow and succeed.

In the next chapter, we will look at the importance of play in young children's lives and how teachers plan for play and playful learning experiences for *all* of the children.

3 The Importance of Play

In chapter 1 I identified the five principles underlying the approach to individualizing curriculum. Here is the second foundational principle:

> 2. Play-based curriculum and playful learning activities are the focus. Teachers plan for play experiences for the children in their care and integrate learning goals taken from early learning standards and/or authentic assessment tools into children's play.

Planning for play experiences is an important part of being an effective early childhood educator. In creating the Developmental Studies that are recommended in this book, teachers plan for and facilitate play so that it is a major part of the curriculum for *all* of the children. They also plan for specific play experiences with individual children's needs in mind.

Support for Play in Children's Lives

There is much support for the importance of play in children's lives. Books and position papers have been published on the benefits of play for children:

- Researchers connect greater academic achievement by children in the primary grades to child-initiated, productive play in the preschool years (Copple and Bredekamp 2009).
- Physical and mental health experts advocate for increased play opportunities for children (Ginsburg 2007) and warn of dire consequences as children become more sedentary and as kindergartens become less playful (Ginsburg 2007; Miller and Almon 2009).

- Developmental psychologists and educational theorists explain the value of adults serving as guides and integrating learning goals in child-directed play so that playful learning is at the heart of curricular practices (Hirsh-Pasek and Golinkoff 2014).

Playful learning is a whole-child approach to education that includes *both* free play and guided play. Guided play offers a new twist. It refers to play in a structured environment around a general curricular goal that is designed to stimulate children's natural curiosity, exploration, and play with learning-oriented materials. In *guided play*, learning remains child-directed. This is a key point. Children learn targeted information through exploration of a well-designed and structured environment . . . and through the support of adults who ask open-ended questions to gently guide the child's exploration. (Hirsh-Pasek and Golinkoff 2014)

To truly delight in young children, to know them well and learn more about them, teachers need to provide multiple opportunities for children to explore, investigate, problem solve, pretend, and play every day in an early childhood program.

Play is essential to development because it contributes to the cognitive, physical, social, and emotional well-being of children and youth. . . . Perhaps above all, play is a simple joy that is a cherished part of childhood. (Ginsburg 2007, 182–83)

In the end the most significant aspect of play is that it allows us to express our joy and connect most deeply with the best in ourselves, and in others. (Brown 2009, 218)

Excellent teachers know . . . it's *both* joy *and* learning. . . . They go hand in hand. . . . Teachers are always more effective when they tap into this natural love of learning rather than dividing work and enjoyment. As some early childhood educators like to put it, children love nothing better than "hard fun." (Copple and Bredekamp 2009, 50)

The Levels of Play

Not all play experiences result in the same benefits for children. Children benefit the most when they are deeply engaged. They are in the flow, not easily distracted, and solve problems without becoming frustrated or overwhelmed. Such play is at a high level. It is not chaotic and out of control, nor is it simplistic or repetitive. It's important that teachers evaluate the level of the children's play. In order to do so, they want to make sure they are familiar with the characteristics of different kinds of play.

In my book *Developmentally Appropriate Play: Guiding Young Children to a Higher Level* (Gronlund 2010), I identify three levels of play:

1 Chaotic or out-of-control play
2 Simplistic and repetitive play
3 High-level, purposeful, complex play

Let's look at the characteristics of each of these kinds of play so that teachers can easily recognize the level of a child's engagement.

Chaotic or out-of-control play

- Children's safety is a concern.
- Their voices are loud and high pitched.
- Children show high levels of physicality, sometimes bordering on dangerous risk-taking behaviors.
- There may be extreme hilarity—children laughing and giggling uncontrollably.
- More disagreements arise and may result in physical injury or in hurt feelings.
- The noise level is high. (Although purposeful play also involves noise and physical activity, a threshold is crossed when it deteriorates into chaotic or out-of-control play.)
- Teachers must employ many techniques and strategies to help children settle down and engage more productively.

Simplistic, repetitive play

- The play is often repetitive and not very involved.
- Safety or noise is rarely an issue, so this play may not always grab the teacher's attention.
- The child may imitate actions but does not go beyond that imitation.
- For toddlers, this type of play is rewarding and appropriate. For preschoolers and kindergartners, however, it is lacking in the qualities of more complex, imaginative play.

High-level, purposeful, complex play

- The play is safe and filled with purpose and meaning.
- It's imaginative. Children use objects for different purposes and creatively solve problems that arise.
- Children's eyes are bright and their energy and engagement are high.
- Children's voices are noisy but not overly so, and they can be easily quieted down if necessary.
- If playing with other children, they are socially successful. They negotiate and compromise with each other independently or with minimal teacher assistance.
- If playing independently, they are deeply focused on what they are doing.
- Children weave into their play concepts they understand and skills they have acquired.
- Children work to sustain the play because it is fun and rewarding.

Planning for High-Level Play

High-level play does not develop on its own. It takes a lot of steps to facilitate and support it. These steps include

- organizing the environment and changing materials as needed,
- allowing plenty of time in the daily schedule for high-level play to develop,
- planning for play with specific learning goals in mind, and
- facilitating play experiences.

The playtime in a toddler, preschool, or kindergarten classroom is not random or haphazard. It is carefully planned and facilitated by the teachers. They have planned the organization of the environment, the available materials, and the procedures for children to work and play within that environment. And they are ever ready to use multiple teaching strategies to help children be successful, grow, and learn.

Some teachers refer to their playtime as "free play." But this label does not reflect the amount of thoughtfulness in teacher planning or the amount of learning benefits for the children. In fact, there are often people (children's family members, administrators, community members, policy makers) who think that "free play" really means a "free-for-all." They may think there is no planning, no teacher intervention, and no purposefulness or learning involved in the play.

Effective early childhood educators know that indeed there is a great deal of planning, teacher involvement, purposefulness, and learning in children's play. Rather than calling playtime "free play," some teachers have renamed this time to reflect its intentionality and importance. What do you and your colleagues call your playtime? Do you think that one of the following titles communicates more clearly what really goes on as children engage in high-level play? You can call playtime:

- investigation time,
- exploration time,
- discovery time,
- activity time,
- choice time,
- focused playtime,
- center time.

Teachers need to consider how best to communicate to others the importance of this time in their daily schedule and name it appropriately.

Another important element that leads to high-level play is the amount of time dedicated to it in the daily schedule. Young children do not settle into high-level play immediately. They need time to check things out, consider possibilities, determine play partners, and get involved. If the time is too brief or they are interrupted, they may hesitate to get deeply engaged. Recommendations for the amount of time for play and exploration both indoors and outdoors are as follows:

- at least sixty minutes of indoor play at learning centers
- daily outdoor play plus opportunities for physical activities and music and movement indoors (Copple and Bredekamp 2009)

Planning for the Environment

A carefully planned environment is one of the primary reasons playtime is not a free-for-all. In early childhood programs, the environment is a very important element of the curriculum.

> Teachers know that the room arrangement and presentation of materials can deeply affect children's behavior. They consider traffic flow and noise levels. . . . The arrangement of furniture and shelves directs children toward the productive use of materials in specific areas. Noise levels are considered so that materials that tend toward greater physical and verbal involvement are placed near each other. Materials that tend toward quieter use are also grouped together. (Gronlund 2013, 105)

Typically, the classroom includes well-defined areas for these activities:

- block building and construction
- dramatic play
- sensory explorations
- artistic creation
- looking at and enjoying books
- writing and drawing
- using manipulative toys for math explorations and fine-motor skill practice

There may be other areas that teachers create as well. They may have a music corner or a science table. Teachers of toddlers may consider the following to be important parts of the environment for their young charges:

- a crawling area and a climbing structure where children can explore their developing gross-motor capabilities
- a rocking chair in which to be snuggled as children develop loving relationships with their caregivers

The environment in early childhood classrooms is structured and planned. Teachers continually observe how well it is being used by the children. If problems arise, changes are made. Perhaps the shelves need to be rearranged so there is more room for the ramps and bridges that children are construct-ing in the block area. Or perhaps more materials need to be made available to children at the math manipulatives area as children combine various materials in extensive sorting and categorizing or pattern-making schemes. Teachers are always observing and reflecting about the success of the play areas and making changes as needed. But these changes do not need to happen every day or even every week. Teachers change things in the environment when the following occurs:

- Children are ignoring an area.
- Children are bored with what is available.
- Children's behavior is not productive in certain areas.
- The teacher determines that a change is needed to support an interest of the children, a developmental need, or a topic of study or project that has emerged. (Gronlund 2013, 111)

Teachers are intentional in making the environment as interesting, inviting, and organized as possible. They add materials and rearrange furniture as they support children's successful engagement in play.

"I have noticed that so many children are interested in building structures in the block area. I realize that I need to provide more tools (such as plastic hammers, saws, and screwdrivers) and more picture books with different block constructions and buildings. I think I'll add writing materials, too, and see what they do with those. I'll encourage them to make signs for their buildings or plans before they build. It ought to be interesting." —Mark

Learning through Play

As children are deeply engaged in high-level play, much learning occurs. Teachers can identify learning goals for play experiences and plan for materials and teacher interactions that build on those goals. They can also reflect on what goals they see children demonstrate as they play. The learning goals can be taken directly from early learning standards or from authentic assessment tools. When completing weekly lesson planning frameworks, teachers identify learning goals in play areas and experiences for *all* of the children. They then plan the appropriate materials and teacher support strategies related to those goals. Here is the first page of a preschool classroom planning framework that is organized so that teachers can relate goals to play areas.

Preschool Weekly Planning and Reflection Framework

Program/School: _____   Date: _____   Teacher(s): _____

Ongoing Project (optional): _____

	Learning goal(s)	Additional materials or focus	Vocabulary words
BLOCKS			
DRAMATIC PLAY			
SENSORY TABLE			
ART			
MANIPULATIVES			
CLASS LIBRARY			
WRITING CENTER			
OTHER CENTER			

You can find a blank copy of all three of the pages of this planning format in appendix B. The second page is used to plan small- and large-group experiences as well as transitions and daily routines. The third page serves as a reflection page for teachers. Examples and guidance for completing this type of planning framework (as well as for infant/toddler and kindergarten ones) can be found in my book *Planning for Play, Observation, and Learning in Preschool and Kindergarten* (Gronlund 2013). I will address more about incorporating learning goals into planning for individual children and how to use the reflection page in later chapters.

> "Even though I plan for learning goals associated with our different play areas and activities, I'm always amazed when children show me what they know related to our goals without me initiating it. Today, during open choice, Annie chose to play with the manipulatives and on her own counted plastic screws. She demonstrated one-to-one correspondence as she counted all the way to nineteen screws!" —Brett

Teachers' Roles in Play

Teacher facilitation is an essential component in high-level play experiences. Teachers are continually observing children at play to determine how best to support the children's play. It's an ongoing dance between teachers and children. When they are observing, teachers are not totally withdrawn from interacting with children. They are ready to step in and out of play experiences, offering support and assistance, problem-solving with the children, providing different materials or ideas, and helping them to engage in high-level play with all of its benefits.

> The goal of play facilitation should always be helping children engage in high-level play rather than only intervening to stop chaotic and out-of-control behavior. . . . Separating children, taking away materials, or ending the play should be an intervention of last resort and should only occur after many other attempts have been made to get the children focused in more productive play. It's an important mind-set for teachers to have. Rather than immediately seeing the play as a behavior problem on the part of the children, teachers should ask themselves, "In what ways can I intervene so that the play changes? What can I offer in the way of ideas, materials, or my involvement that will provide safety and control?" (Gronlund 2010, 19–20)

When teachers see simplistic, repetitive play (especially with preschoolers), they also step in and facilitate.

When teachers observe children engaged in simplistic play, they need to help them move beyond the repetitive actions and get engaged so that their intellect is more challenged. This may mean responding as one might to a toddler, adding vocabulary and providing descriptive commentary as the child repeats actions. Or a teacher may add suggestions or materials, posing questions that lead the child into a higher level as they pretend or use symbolic thinking. (Gronlund 2010, 21)

As children play, teachers are observers, facilitators, and even coplayers. And at all times, they are ever ready to step back and turn the play over to the children. Throughout this book, we will continue to explore ways to facilitate play, especially with individual children in mind.

Conclusion

Play-based curriculum and playful learning are foundational principles in creating Developmental Studies and individualizing curriculum. Teachers plan the daily schedule so that there is ample time for play, organize and structure the play environment, plan for play experiences with goals in mind, and choose among a variety of roles to support children's play. In the next chapter, I will discuss the importance of learning about children's interests and favorite activities and how this information can influence planning for play.

> "I want my kindergarten classroom to be more playful. I'm very drawn to projects and think those would be really interesting and way more meaningful for the children. This documentation is pushing me to figure out ways to offer more open-ended activities at my choice time." —Kelly

Learning about Children's Interests and Favorite Activities

Early childhood educators are much more successful in engaging children when they are familiar with the children's interests.

Consider the following:

- Children are more motivated when they are interested in something.
- Children will tackle harder challenges when they are interested.
- Children will stay focused longer on something in which they are interested.

Teachers will be able to capture much more of the children's attention when the children are interested. Behavior problems lessen with increased motivation, and children's opportunities to demonstrate and practice their developmental capabilities will be heightened. Planning curricular activities based on children's interests is a "win-win" approach—good for the children and good for the teachers.

Here are some examples of children expressing their interests and favorite activities.

"I love playdough. It's my favorite!" Lupita smiles broadly as she mushes the playdough between her hands. Her teacher, Mary, has noticed that Lupita chooses playdough almost every time it is available.

Josiah often plays in the pretend kitchen in his toddler classroom. "I cook," he says as he bangs a wooden spoon inside a metal pot. "Me make soup." He stirs and bangs and offers the "soup" to his teachers and to other children. The other children mimic their teachers, blowing on and sipping from Josiah's outstretched spoon as he grins broadly.

> "When can we build the marble run again, Mr. Mark?" Mallory and Todd ask this question almost daily. Todd touches Mallory's arm gently as he says to his friend, "We wanna make the marbles go really fast, huh, Mallory?" Mallory nods her head and smiles. Mr. Mark has noticed that these two will play for up to forty minutes at a time when the marble run is available.

Young children who are given the opportunity to choose from among a variety of play areas and activities will demonstrate interests and choose favorites. As teachers observe these choices and identify trends in the children's engagement, they can learn a lot about each child. Children tend to choose activities that engage them. And, usually, they are more fully engaged by activities and play experiences in which they can use their developmental strengths. Let's learn more about the strengths of the children described above.

> Lupita's fine-motor skills are strong. She can easily pick up small items whether in play or at snacktimes and mealtimes. She is successful as she makes marks with crayons and pencils, and comfortably holds these drawing/writing tools in a pincer grasp. She loves to explore with her sense of touch—the messier the better for her. She loves the cool, soft feel of playdough in her hands. She often chooses to play with sand and water, noticing the different ways the textures feel as she plunges her hands into whatever is in the sensory table. And she fingerpaints freely, spreading the paint up her arms and over the backs of her hands, as well as swiping her hands in broad strokes across the shiny fingerpaint paper.

> Josiah engages in pretend play often. He already has a sense of the abstract and is comfortable with the unseen and imagined. He knows there is no soup in his pot. When he pretends to cook or care for the baby dolls, he is imitating adult roles. He uses language to describe what he is doing and to communicate to others. Pretend play allows him to feel successful, to engage with both adults and other children, and to explore what it means to be a daddy or a mommy in his world.

Todd and Mallory are developing a deep friendship based on a mutual interest. They are successful with the marble run because they have a sense of how to engineer the plastic pieces in order to create a ramp with a sufficient angle for the marble to run smoothly and with speed. Together they problem solve, experiment, reconfigure, and evaluate their success. They persist when it doesn't work, assisting each other in sticking with the task at hand, overcoming obstacles, and creatively combining pieces in new ways so that the path of the marble is more interesting.

In contrast to choosing favorites based on their strengths, children may avoid activities and play experiences in which they have to use skills that are not as strong. Children with strong gross-motor skills may avoid fine-motor activities that are more challenging for them. Children who have not developed social skills or the language to communicate effectively with others may avoid dramatic play experiences. They may not feel confident negotiating roles in pretend play. They may play alone or off to the side of groups who are actively interacting, using materials, and taking on various pretend roles.

Determining and Documenting Children's Interests

How then can teachers best determine children's interests? How can they learn more about children's favorite activities? Here are two ways:

1 They ask children outright.
2 They observe children over time to see what choices they make and where they spend time in engaged and productive activity.

For our Developmental Study, we are going to use two different forms of documentation to learn more about what children choose to engage in most frequently:

1 The Child Interest Survey
2 The Child Choice Record

Let's consider the most effective ways to use these two types of documentation to gain information about children's interests and choices.

The Child Interest Survey

The Child Interest Survey is used to ask a child directly about her interests. This format is especially successful with children who can show and/or discuss what they enjoy most. Here is a copy of the blank form. You can find a blank copy of this form in appendix B or download a PDF version from www.redleafpress.org.

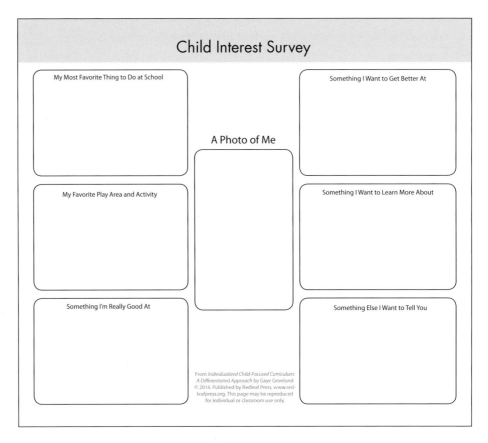

To complete the Child Interest Survey, the teacher interviews the child and asks her to tell and/or show what she likes to do in the classroom. The teacher writes down the child's responses and photographs her demonstrating what she likes to do most. There are six questions on the survey:

1 What is your most favorite thing to do at school?
2 What is your favorite play area or activity?
3 What is something you are really good at?
4 What is something you want to get better at?
5 What is something you want to learn more about?
6 Is there something else you want to tell me?

Here are two completed examples of Child Interest Surveys. The first one documents the interests of a three-year-old who demonstrated rather than discussed her responses. You can see that the teacher took photographs and inserted them into the form and then added descriptions of what the child was showing her.

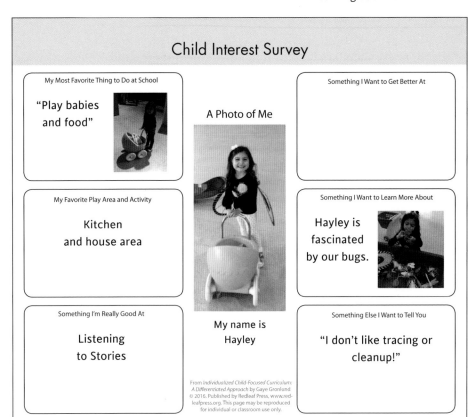

Child Interest Survey

My Most Favorite Thing to Do at School

"Play babies and food"

My Favorite Play Area and Activity

Kitchen
and house area

Something I'm Really Good At

Listening
to Stories

A Photo of Me

My name is
Hayley

Something I Want to Get Better At

Something I Want to Learn More About

Hayley is
fascinated
by our bugs.

Something Else I Want to Tell You

"I don't like tracing or
cleanup!"

From *Individualized Child-Focused Curriculum: A Differentiated Approach* by Gaye Gronlund © 2016. Published by Redleaf Press, www.redleafpress.org. This page may be reproduced for individual or classroom use only.

The second example shows the statements made by a four-year-old who could describe and discuss his interests more fully. Notice that once again the teacher included a photograph. This photo showing the child in action adds more richness to the survey.

Child Interest Survey

My Most Favorite Thing to Do at School

"I like to play in home living and make a house in the block area. I make airplanes with Legos."

My Favorite Play Area and Activity

"I go to the computer and play the food game. And I color pictures, like a house. I like to count my numbers to 100!"

Something I'm Really Good At

"Lacing and making stuff with Legos and coloring people and houses but not coloring like in library books."

A Photo of Me

My name is
Mason

Something I Want to Get Better At

"Reading words out of books and writing words and picking my colors and face painting."

Something I Want to Learn More About

"Listening to the teacher and the alphabet song and drawing my letters."

Something Else I Want to Tell You

"Reading books, making a plant, and drawing animals."

From *Individualized Child-Focused Curriculum: A Differentiated Approach* by Gaye Gronlund © 2016. Published by Redleaf Press, www.redleafpress.org. This page may be reproduced for individual or classroom use only.

Each survey should reflect the unique interests of the child. That is why it's important to interview each child individually rather than in a small group with other children. When young children are interviewed in a group, they are sometimes influenced by what other children say or do, and the survey does not reflect the child's true interests. Adding photographs to the survey makes it more interesting and authentic. Teachers should be sure to have the camera handy so they can take photographs if the child wants to show what he likes to do. They can also invite the child to draw something in answer to the interview questions. Here are two drawings that children created in response to their teacher's questions.

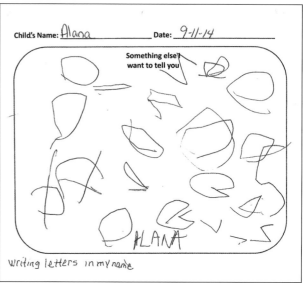

You can also review examples of completed Child Interest Surveys in the Developmental Studies in appendix A.

"I had to do a lot of prompting to get her to elaborate about her favorite activities and interests. But everything she told me was in line with what the family said about her interests when we completed the Individual Child Information Record." —Brett

"I was amazed that even our two-year-olds were able to tell us things they were interested in." —Linda

The Child Choice Record

The Child Interest Survey is not always successful as a way to capture children's interests. If the child is reluctant to converse, hesitant to demonstrate, or says things like "I don't know," this interview format may not be the most informative. If that is the case, teachers will want to observe the child over time and note the areas of the classroom and the activities to which she gravitates more frequently. They can track children's choices as they play and work at the learning areas in their classroom on the Child Choice Record.

Here are blank copies of the Toddler, Preschool, and Kindergarten Child Choice Records. You will see that the play/learning areas are slightly different to reflect the differences in typical curricular approaches for the three age groups. You can find full-sized copies of these formats in appendix B or go to www.redleafpress.org to download PDF versions.

Toddler Choice Record

(may be used to tally one child's choices or a group of children's choices)

Date _____   Child(ren) _____

_____

Paint Easel	Blocks	Play House
Manipulatives	**Crawling Area**	**Climbing Structure**
Book Corner	**Sensory Table**	**Rocking Chair**

Preschool Choice Record

(may be used to tally one child's choices or a group of children's choices)

Child(ren): _____   Date: _____

Art	Blocks	Dramatic Play
Manipulatives	Science/Math	Music/Movement
Library	Sensory Table	Writing Center

Kindergarten Choice Record

(may be used to tally one child's choices or a group of children's choices)

Child(ren): _____   Date: _____

Listening Center	Dramatic Play	Journaling Center	Alphabet Center	Flannel Board or Pocket Charts
Class Library	Writing Center	Blocks	Math Activity	Sensory Table
Art	Manipulatives	Science Exploration	Informational Reading	Math and Science Journaling

It's best for teachers to record children's choices over a one-week period or longer. In this way, they can pay attention to the areas and activities in which children become truly engaged rather than the areas that children visit briefly. Teachers will want to discuss with their colleagues how they will determine whether a child is engaged or not. They may decide on a certain amount of time as an indicator: "When the child stays at an area using the materials in a productive way for ten minutes or more, we will note it on the choice record." Or they can identify specific observations that show whether children are truly engaged or not: What do they see in the child's facial expressions, body language, and use of materials? What do they hear the child say, whether to a teacher or to another child?

Look at the following photograph. What leads you to conclude that this child was indeed engaged in this block play?

Perhaps you identified how many blocks were used to create a complex structure across a fairly extensive amount of space. Or you may have noted how the blocks were placed at different levels, which took some problem solving on the part of the child. You may have identified that the girl in the photo is unaware of the camera and looks deeply engaged in what she is doing. Let's consider the signs of engagement more fully.

When truly engaged, children look . . .
bright eyed, focused, smiling, intent. (What else might you add?)

When truly engaged, children sound . . .
excited, enthusiastic, questioning, wondering, laughing, joyous.
(What else might you add?)

When truly engaged, children say . . .
"I love this." "I like to . . ." "Can we do more?" "What else can we do
with . . ." "Can I stay longer?" "Can [another child] play too?" "Look what
I did, Teacher!" "Teacher, can you help us?" (What else might you add?)

When truly engaged, teachers see children . . .
try different ways to use the materials; work through problems
that arise on their own or seek help from a peer or teacher; use their
imaginations and creativity; apply skills that they already have or
practice skills that they are learning; work independently with great
focus; work cooperatively with others to continue the experience. (What
else might you add?)

As teachers observe for children's engagement and record their choices of play areas and activities on the Child Choice Record, they continue to act as play facilitators. As I stated in the previous chapter, they are ready to step in and out of play experiences, offering support and assistance, engaging in problem solving with the children, providing different materials or ideas, and helping them to engage in high-level play with all of its benefits.

COMPLETING CHILD CHOICE RECORDS

Teachers can decide how best to record information about children's choices. They can write children's full names or just their initials in the appropriate boxes for the areas where they get engaged productively. They can also include the amount of time each child stays working in that area or at that activity. The time does not need to be determined to the second or the minute—no stopwatch is needed! However, it should be a good approximation of the time the child was involved. Here are two examples of completed Child Choice Records. You can also review examples of completed Child Choice Records in the Developmental Studies in appendix A.

Toddler Choice Record

(may be used to tally one child's choices or a group of children's choices)

Date 9/30 – 10/5   Child(ren) Hayley, Steven, Andre, Maleesa, Nicole, Tyler

Paint Easel	Blocks	Play House
H: IIII	H:	H: IIII I
S:	S: IIII	S:
A:	A: III	A: I
M: II	M:	M: II
N: I	N: II	N: III
T: II	T: III	T: II

Manipulatives	Crawling Area	Climbing Structure
H: II	H:	H: I
S: III	S: IIII	S: III
A: II	A: III	A: IIII
M: I	M:	M: I
N:	N:	N:
T: I	T: II	T: II

Book Corner	Sensory Table	Rocking Chair
H: III	H: I	H: II
S: III	S: I	S: I
A:	A:	A:
M: IIII I	M:	M: IIII
N: IIII	N: I	N: III
T: I	T:	T:

Preschool Choice Record

(may be used to tally one child's choices or a group of children's choices)

Child(ren): Mason, Danielle, Kevin, and Erin   Date: 10/7-17

Art	Blocks	Dramatic Play
M: I	M: IIIIII (making pizza store)	M: II
D:	D: III (making pizza store)	D: II
K:	K:	K: III
E: III	E:	E: I

Manipulatives	Science/Math	Music/Movement
Playdough	Gourds	M: I
M: IIII (making pizzas)	M: III	D: I
D: III (making pizzas)	D: IIII	K: I
K: II (making pizzas)	K: II	E:
E: IIII (making cupcakes and pastries)	E:	

Library	Sensory Table	Writing Center
M:	M: II	M: IIII
D:	D: I	D: II (practicing letters with dry erase markers)
K:	K:	K: IIII
E:	E: II	E: II (dry erase markers)

Teachers may want to consider completing choice records every month or two so they can note trends in children's engagement or changes in their choices. Teachers report that these records help them to conduct research (as I have discussed) about individual children.

> "I was surprised to see that Curtis sticks to an activity for a long time, so there were only a few marks on the choice record for him. He doesn't move much. He writes a lot and plays in dramatic play often. Those are his favorites." —Jordan

> "In completing the choice record, I noticed Devin spent a lot of time in transitional areas, lots of time in the bathroom, cleaning up. He surprised me. I pictured him busier and more engaged. Now I realize that he likes sensory things." —Jarrod

Conclusion

Child Choice Records can also help teachers evaluate how fully play areas are being used by *all* of the children or how successful specific activities are. These records, then, help them reflect on their planning and consider what changes might need to be made. For example, if they notice that very few children are choosing an area or activity, they may plan for something different there. They might consider

- going to the area themselves and modeling ways to engage with the materials,
- serving as a helpmate to children as they participate in the activity,
- changing the materials available in the area, or
- changing the activity completely so that something new and different is available.

Interest surveys and choice records give teachers information about individual children and help them evaluate the success of their planning for the environment and for specific activities. In the next chapter, we will look at planning for play experiences with the interests of individual children in mind.

> "I feel this is at the heart of teaching—looking at the individual children, looking at their interests and what they can do. It feels really good to me. It's the basis for good teaching." —Sara

Planning for Play Based on Children's Interests

Once teachers have determined the children's interests, their next step is to plan play experiences that take advantage of the children's natural motivation and willingness to engage more fully. In chapter 3, we recognized that teachers plan for high-level play for *all* of the children by arranging and provisioning the environment and engaging in a variety of play facilitation strategies. In this chapter, we will look at how to individualize those plans.

Recall that children benefit more from the play experience when they are truly engaged. Teachers can weave in learning goals more easily and behavior problems are lessened. Planning based on children's interests makes teachers' jobs easier and children far more successful.

Approaches to Learning

In the early childhood years, teachers are helping children learn to be learners. They are preparing children for academic success throughout their school careers. In many state early learning standards, approaches to learning are identified as a domain of development that stands alone. In others, they are incorporated into the social/emotional domain. The developers of standards recognize the importance of helping children develop their approaches to learning in the early years. Research studies have connected such approaches to long-term benefits for children's academic careers as well as for the development of skills they will use throughout their lives. Let's explore these approaches to learning more fully.

Approaches to learning for young children are defined as the "inclinations, dispositions, and learning styles in using their knowledge and skills to interact with their learning environment" (Conn-Powers 2006, 1). The conclusions of the National Educational Goals Panel (1995) state that they are a key component in school readiness and include the following six learning outcomes:

1 Curiosity/Initiative
2 Persistence
3 Attention
4 Self-direction
5 Problem solving
6 Creativity (Conn-Powers 2006, 2)

Here are some descriptions of children engaged in high-level play. Consider the approaches to learning that they are demonstrating. As you read each description, look at the list above and determine which ones of the six approaches each child is showing.

> Kayla and two other children worked together to build a structure with floor toys, sharing materials and ideas. At one point, one child suggested they add a roof. Kayla said, "Great idea!" and suggested they build it out of magnet blocks. The other child agreed. On their first attempt, the roof immediately collapsed. Kayla said, "Let's try it again." The second time they built a sturdy roof that stood. They continued building structures for approximately twenty minutes.

What approaches to learning did Kayla use in this play experience? She showed self-direction and initiative in coming up with the idea to use the magnet blocks and creativity in creating a structure. She persisted even when the roof collapsed and problem solved to make it sturdier. She showed focused attention in the time she spent on the task.

> Jazlyn chose to go to dramatic play today and was making a restaurant with several other children. Paper, note cards, and writing tools were out and available for them to use. After a few minutes in the restaurant, Jazlyn announced that she had an idea. She took a note card to a table and worked on it for about eight minutes. When she was finished she brought the card over to me and said, "Look, a mouse-sized menu!" She had folded the card in half to create a book. On the front was a picture of a mouse and inside were drawings of food. She said, "It's a menu reserved for mouses! They can order jelly beans, chocolate milk, and pumpkin pie." She continued to add more pages to the menu for approximately ten minutes.

What approaches to learning did Jazlyn use in this play experience? She demonstrated initiative in coming up with the idea for the book and self-direction and creativity in making it. She problem solved to fold the card and make a small book-like menu and showed focused attention throughout.

Another important aspect of children's development that overlaps with approaches to learning is the development of self-regulation: the ability of children to think before they act, to plan, and to have some control over their thoughts, feelings, and behavior (McClelland and Tominey 2014).

> Self-regulation can be defined as the integration of . . . executive function skills into behavior. In other words, the components of executive function help children learn how to consciously and effectively manage their behavior so that they can work and play well with other children, follow directions, calm themselves down when they get upset, remember instructions, and persist on difficult tasks. (McClelland and Tominey 2014, 3)

The components of executive function to which these authors refer are similar to some of the approaches to learning identified above. Here are the three components of executive function:

1   Attentional or cognitive flexibility—the ability to focus and pay attention to a task, to ignore distractions, and to switch to another task when needed
2   Working memory—the ability to hold and process information mentally
3   Inhibitory control—the ability to stop an impulse and to choose another response (McClelland and Tominey 2014, 2–3)

Let's think about self-regulation as we consider children's engagement in high-level play. As you read each of these descriptions of children at play, identify how each child is showing self-regulation.

During center time, Dylan approached a small group of children playing. "What are you guys building?" he asked. The children told him they were building a city so they could drive race cars through it. Dylan asked, "Cool! Can I play?" One of the boys said, "Sure, you can build the roads." Dylan jumped in and began building a parking lot. "We can keep the cars here until the road is built," he said. He used various-sized block pieces to outline the lot. Everyone worked together to place the cars there, and Dylan counted, touching each car as he did so. "There's twenty-one cars, guys!" he said. Another child came over and stepped on the parking lot, forcing the pieces apart. Dylan remained calm and said, "Hey, you stepped on my parking lot. Can you help me fix it?" The two worked together to fix the structure, and Dylan began building the road.

How did Dylan show self-regulation? He managed his own behavior in order to join the other children in their already established play. He showed working memory about parking lots and in maintaining the quantity as he counted the twenty-one cars. He demonstrated impulse control when the structure was disturbed by the other child and flexible thinking in asking the child to help him rebuild.

> Brandon often plays a game he calls "sea monster" that he made up on the playground. Today he asked some other children if they wanted to play the game with him. They agreed, and Brandon explained how to play. "All you have to do is run and scream to get away from the invisible sea monster." All of the other children took off running except for one. Brandon walked over to him and asked, "Why are you just standing here?" The child explained that he was afraid of the sea monster. Brandon told him not to worry, that it was just pretend, and then took him by the hand and they ran off together.

How did Brandon show self-regulation? He managed his behavior to play well with other children, set out directions for the group, and then followed them. He showed cognitive flexibility by switching to the task of comforting his friend and inhibited his own behavior by not immediately running away, instead talking with the child, and then engaging in the sea monster play with him.

How Approaches to Learning Lead to Academic Success

The most exciting thing about emphasizing approaches to learning and self-regulation is that research now directly connects them to children's future academic success!

> There is research that suggests strong links between positive approaches to learning and children's success in school. For example, one study found that children with higher levels of attentiveness, task persistence, eagerness to learn, learning independence, flexibility, and organization, generally did better in literacy and math at the end of the kindergarten school year and the beginning of their first grade year. In addition, children who approach learning tasks or novel situations with these positive approaches to learning are better able to regulate their learning experiences, and more quickly acquire general knowledge and cognitive skills. (Conn-Powers 2006, 2)

The development of self-regulation helps children not only in school but throughout their lives.

Research has shown that strong self-regulation relates to positive social and academic outcomes early on and throughout a child's life. . . . Specifically, studies show that children's self-regulation abilities in preschool relate to later school outcomes [including higher reading and math scores, greater odds of completing college] and predict future schooling decisions, wages, and even employment. . . . Self-regulation is also important for social outcomes. . . . One study . . . predicted lower criminality, increased financial status, and better physical and mental health outcomes in adulthood. (McClelland and Tominey 2014, 2–3)

Therefore, when teachers plan for play, they are building on children's strengths as well as strengthening their approaches to learning and self-regulation. When they plan for experiences that deeply engage children, they are building children's future academic skills just as much, if not more so, as when they teach children alphabet letters or help them understand quantities. And they are helping children to build not only learning skills for school but also skills that will benefit them throughout their lives.

Individualized Play Planning

For our Developmental Study, we are going to use a format called the Individualized Play Planning Sheet. To complete this plan, you will refer to the Child Interest Survey and the results of your Child Choice Records. Then you will plan for play activities that will build on children's interests and favorites, thus knowing that you are developing their approaches to learning as well. Here is a copy of the blank form. You can find a blank copy of this format in appendix B or download a PDF version from www.redleafpress.org.

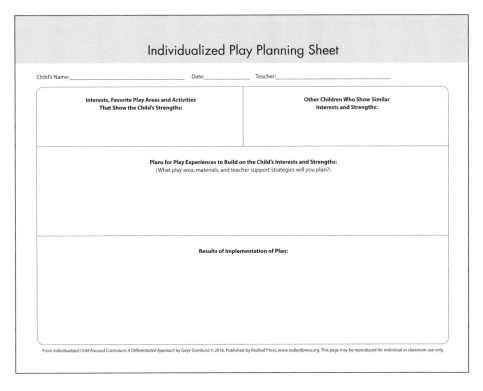

Individualized Play Planning Sheet

Child's Name:_____   Date:_____   Teacher:_____

Interests, Favorite Play Areas and Activities That Show the Child's Strengths:	Other Children Who Show Similar Interests and Strengths:

Plans for Play Experiences to Build on the Child's Interests and Strengths:
(What play area, materials, and teacher support strategies will you plan?)

Results of Implementation of Plan:

From *Individualized Child-Focused Curriculum: A Differentiated Approach* by Gaye Gronlund © 2016. Published by Redleaf Press, www.redleafpress.org. This page may be reproduced for individual or classroom use only.

You can see that this play plan has some unique features. There are places for the teacher to identify and record

- the child's strengths by noting his interests, favorite play areas, and favorite activities;
- the names of other children who have shown similar interests and strengths and might benefit from this plan;
- a plan for play experiences that builds on the child's interests and strengths;
- the play area(s), materials, and teacher support strategies that would work best with that plan.

All of the above items are completed *before* implementing the plan. Then teachers observe as children engage in the play experience(s) and note the results of the implementation for both the individual child and the additional children identified on the planning sheet.

> "The Play Planning Sheets have helped as a great guide. They make the teacher sit back and think. He thinks about a few individual children and then beyond them to the rest of the class. He looks more deeply at his lesson planning." —Teresa

Let's look at two completed examples of Individualized Play Planning Sheets. These completed examples do not include the results of the implementation of these plans. We will look at those results later in this chapter.

Individualized Play Planning Sheet

Child's Name: Henry   Date: 10-11   Teacher: Kristin

Interests, Favorite Play Areas and Activities That Show the Child's Strengths:
Legos, Blocks, Cars and Trucks

Other Children Who Show Similar Interests and Strengths:
Kevin, Jason, and Oliver

Plans for Play Experiences to Build on the Child's Interests and Strengths:
(What play area, materials, and teacher support strategies will you plan?)

With teacher support, children can count, sort, and build with the various blocks and Legos provided.

Add books about counting and building.

Results of Implementation of Plan:

For this child:

For the other children:

Individualized Play Planning Sheet

Child's Name: __Alana__   Date: __12/8__   Teacher: __CeCe__

Interests, Favorite Play Areas and Activities That Show the Child's Strengths:	Other Children Who Show Similar Interests and Strengths:
Reading, Writing, Dramatic Area, and Art Zone	Kevin, Jason, and Oliver

Plans for Play Experiences to Build on the Child's Interests and Strengths:
(What play area, materials, and teacher support strategies will you plan?)

Plan to bring more writing materials (crayons, markers, papers) and books to dramatic play.

Set up dramatic play as a restaurant with menus, ordering pads, etc.

Results of Implementation of Plan:

For this child:

For the other children:

You can also review examples of completed Individualized Play Planning Sheets in the Developmental Studies in appendix A.

> "The Individualized Play Planning Sheet was my favorite. It got at what was most important. I'm thinking, 'What am I going to do in the room based on what I know about this child?' Sometimes there are so many layers—this one, this format made me feel most satisfied. This was just for me. I was working with the kids. And then I was thinking who else this would impact. I'd love to have this in my weekly planning and just have this to think about. We could work as a team and each of us could look at half of the kids and think about how we're differentiating for specific children." —Sara

The Plan Is Not for All Children

A teacher does not need to complete an Individualized Play Planning Sheet for every child. It's not appropriate to say that *every* child will benefit from the same plan because not all children share the same interests and strengths. Neither of the examples shown above stated that *all* of the children shared similar interests and strengths. The teachers were thoughtful and specific about which children would benefit from the plan. They got their data or information for these conclusions from the interest surveys and choice records. They engaged in the research I described in chapter 1. This is the first step in individualization for teachers: reflecting on observations and information gathered about individual children. And for individualized play planning, they analyze the surveys and choice records, looking for the following:

1   The interests expressed by different children in the surveys
2   The play areas and materials chosen by different children as consistent favorites
3   Trends that show which children have similar interests and strengths

Once this study and reflection has taken place, teachers complete two to four Individualized Play Planning Sheets that address the interests of the small groups of children they have identified.

Let's study two different choice records and identify such trends that would lead to effective play planning.

Toddler Choice Record

(may be used to tally one child's choices or a group of children's choices)

Date 9/30 – 10/5   Child(ren) Hayley, Steven, Andre, Maleesa, Nicole, Tyler

Paint Easel	Blocks	Play House
H: IIII	H:	H: IIII I
S:	S: IIIII	S:
A:	A: III	A: I
M: II	M:	M: II
N: I	N: II	N: III
T: II	T: III	T: II

Manipulatives	Crawling Area	Climbing Structure
H: II	H:	H: I
S: III	S: IIIII	S: III
A: II	A: III	A: IIIII
M: I	M:	M: I
N:	N:	N:
T: I	T: II	T: II

Book Corner	Sensory Table	Rocking Chair
H: III	H: I	H: II
S: III	S: I	S: I
A:	A:	A:
M: IIIII I	M:	M: IIII
N: IIII	N: I	N: III
T: I	T:	T:

From *Focused Observations: How to Observe Young Children for Assessment and Curriculum Planning*, Second Edition by Gaye Gronlund and Marlyn James, © 2013. Published by Redleaf Press, www.redleafpress.org. This page may be reproduced for individual or classroom use only.

Haley shows some favorites in her choices: Paint Easel, Play House, and Book Corner. Maleesa and Nicole often choose the Book Corner as well, and they both love the rocking chair with or without an adult.

Steven shows some favorites in his choices: Blocks, Crawling Area, and Climbing Structure. Andre often chooses the same three areas. Tyler moves around to other areas more but does engage in these three also.

Individualized Play Planning Sheet

Child's Name: __Steven__   Date: __10/8__   Teacher: __Becky__

Interests, Favorite Play Areas and Activities That Show the Child's Strengths:	Other Children Who Show Similar Interests and Strengths:
Blocks, Crawling Area, Climbing Structure	Andre and Tyler

Plans for Play Experiences to Build on the Child's Interests and Strengths:
(What play area, materials, and teacher support strategies will you plan?)

Encourage the three boys to work cooperatively on building structures in the block area. Maybe create an obstacle course with hollow blocks that could include stepping up and over, climbing, crawling through, and other physical activities. Have them take turns giving children directions to go through the obstacle course.

Provide photos of interesting architecture around the world (Eiffel Tower, Stonehenge, Guggenheim Museum, pyramids, Golden Gate Bridge, etc.) and invite boys to create their own architectural structures.

Results of Implementation of Plan:

For this child:

For the other children:

Individualized Play Planning Sheet

Child's Name: __Hayley__   Date: __10/8__   Teacher: __Becky__

Interests, Favorite Play Areas and Activities That Show the Child's Strengths:	Other Children Who Show Similar Interests and Strengths:
Paint Easel, Play House, Book Corner	Maleesa and Nicole

Plans for Play Experiences to Build on the Child's Interests and Strengths:
(What play area, materials, and teacher support strategies will you plan?)

Add books to the art area with examples of painters' styles (Picasso, pointillists, watercolorists?) and review with Hayley to encourage her to try different styles of painting.
Add books to the play house and model for and encourage girls to read to the baby dolls and to each other.
Observe and script the girls' dramatic play and make a book about it for them to read (add photos?).
Add a basket of books to the rocking chair area for snuggling and reading.

Results of Implementation of Plan:

For this child:

For the other children:

Preschool Choice Record

(may be used to tally one child's choices or a group of children's choices)

Child(ren): Mason, Danielle, Kevin, Erin

Date: 9/30–10/4

Art	Blocks	Dramatic Play
Mason: I Danielle: III Kevin: Erin: II	Mason: IIII Danielle: III Kevin: III Erin:	Mason: I Danielle: II Kevin: Erin: II
Manipulatives	**Science/Math**	**Music/Movement**
Playdough: Mason: IIII Danielle: IIII Kevin: III Erin: III	Mason: I Danielle: I Kevin: Erin:	N.A.
Library	**Sensory Table**	**Writing Center**
Mason: I Danielle: I Kevin: Erin: II	N.A.	Dry Erase Board and Markers: Mason: III Danielle: IIII Kevin: III Erin: III

Mason led the effort to make a pizza store, building the structure in the Blocks and making playdough pizzas to sell there. Danielle and Kevin joined him either at Blocks or playdough or both. All three also showed great interest in the dry erase markers at the Writing Center.

Erin was not interested in the pizzas but made her own cupcakes and pastries. She, too, was interested in the dry erase markers at the Writing Center.

Individualized Play Planning Sheet

Child's Name:__Mason_____   Date:__10/20_____   Teacher:__Jill_____

Interests, Favorite Play Areas and Activities That Show the Child's Strengths:	Other Children Who Show Similar Interests and Strengths:
Blocks, playdough, dramatic play around pizza shop	Danielle and Kevin

Plans for Play Experiences to Build on the Child's Interests and Strengths:
(What play area, materials, and teacher support strategies will you plan?)

In response to Mason's interest, we're opening up "a pizza shop." He's very proud that everyone's following his interests. He's very self-motivated. He got the number cards and organized them to price the pizzas. We'll provide a cash register, order pads, and writing materials so Mason and others can set up and act out the pizza shop. We'll also investigate pizza toppings and help children cut out pictures from magazines to make menus and make word cards for them to copy or use with different topping names (pepperoni, cheese, peppers, olives, ham, pineapple, etc.).

Results of Implementation of Plan:

For this child:

For the other children:

Individualized Play Planning Sheet

Child's Name:__Erin_____   Date:__10/20_____   Teacher:__Jill_____

Interests, Favorite Play Areas and Activities That Show the Child's Strengths:	Other Children Who Show Similar Interests and Strengths:
Playdough—making cupcakes and pastries, writing, sensory table	Malia? Sophie? Juliette?

Plans for Play Experiences to Build on the Child's Interests and Strengths:
(What play area, materials, and teacher support strategies will you plan?)

Erin is not interested in the pizza shop but is making her own cupcakes and pastries. We'll provide her with number cards, cash register, order pads, and writing materials as well, so she can set up a bakery. We'll encourage her to work with other children rather than just on her own, pairing her with Malia, Sophie, or Juliette, who seem to be interested as well. And we'll see if there is any way to integrate the pizza shop and bakery play!

Results of Implementation of Plan:

For this child:

For the other children:

"The choice records helped us think about children as individuals
and to think about their strengths and interests, and that led us to
individualization. We focused on three different children, and each one
has at least one other child in the classroom who is very similar and
benefits from the plans we make. We can immediately apply what we're
thinking of for one child to other children." —Sara

Determining Play Areas, Materials, and Teacher Support Strategies

It's important to keep in mind that curriculum in early childhood classrooms is so much more than what can be found in one curriculum guide, in one framework, or in one set of materials. As teachers plan curriculum for *all* children and adapt aspects of it for *individual* children using the Individualized Play Planning Sheets, they are thinking about multiple things. In this section, we will focus on the following three:

1 The way the classroom environment is organized into play and learning areas
2 The materials that are available to the children in each of these areas
3 The teacher support strategies that will facilitate children's engagement in high-level play and playful learning

Teachers think of these three aspects of curriculum and how they will best meet the needs of all the children, and they think of how to build on the interests of individuals and small groups of children.

Here is a kindergarten teacher's description of her response to an interest demonstrated by a group of children. Read through this description and consider the ways this teacher looked at the three aspects of curriculum listed above.

"I have noticed that many of the children are really gravitating to the writing center. They will choose to go there over anything else. On their own initiative, they make signs and books about the weather. I am really amazed at their interest and enthusiasm. But sometimes it gets too crowded and either behavior problems arise or not all children who want to can participate. So I decided to bring writing into all of the other play and investigation areas. At the sensory table, I had snow that I had collected from outside along with magnifying glasses and watercolor paints. So I puzzled about how to extend it and decided to provide paper, writing tools, and clipboards so that they could write about what they observed and draw a picture. Then I suggested that they could read what they had written to the class at our group meeting. That hooked a few more into writing!" —Kelly

How is Kelly organizing the classroom environment? She already had a well-provisioned writing center in her classroom. She provided a table area with several chairs. She also had a sensory table where she regularly changed out the opportunities for children to explore various items. In this description, snow had been placed in the sensory table.

How is Kelly providing engaging materials? The writing center included shelves and baskets with writing materials, including different kinds of papers (both lined and unlined) and writing utensils (markers, crayons, pencils, and pens). In addition, she had a stapler ready for making books. Cards with the children's names as well as some favorite words were available. At the sensory table, magnifying glasses were provided for children to observe and study the snow. Kelly also offered watercolor paints so that children could change the color of the snow and continue their observations related to the changes that brought about. You can see above that she then decided to expand writing opportunities in the classroom and did so at the sensory table, placing writing materials there along with the always-enticing clipboards (which young children seem to love!).

What teacher support strategies is Kelly using? She encouraged children to write about their observations related to the snow placed in the table. Her support was in the form of presenting an idea and then being ready to guide the children as they recorded their observations. She also gave them another purpose for their writing—the opportunity to share it with others at meeting time. Again, she was ready to help them with that process later in the day.

Kelly's story illustrates a teacher's responsiveness to a group of children—not necessarily the whole group, but the group that showed the most interest in writing. This is a form of individualization just as much as planning for the interests of one child. And, when teachers evaluate trends and plan for groups in this way, they may find it easier to meet the needs of multiple children at one time.

"We found in our lesson plans that we could identify materials that would support the interest of one child but that it ended up helping many others as well. One of the twins likes to be in the mother role in the drama zone. So we put more clothes in there for the girls. We also put appointment books, pencils and paper, and books. Now, several girls are making appointments to take the babies to the doctor and reading to the babies." —LaVonne

Addressing Children with a Specific Expertise

Teachers are sometimes challenged as to how best to respond to an individual child's interests. They often have children in their classrooms who are experts in certain specialized topics. Sometimes these children almost seem obsessive in their interests. The dinosaur expert talks on and on, naming all of the different dinosaurs and describing their similarities and differences, wanting to play only with dinosaur figures, read dinosaur books, complete dinosaur puzzles, and draw dinosaurs. The train expert wants to play with the train set every day or consistently builds trains out of the manipulatives available in the classroom. The princess expert enacts various fairy tales or movie scripts, dressing in anything from the dramatic play area that can serve as a costume and directing others to act out the story correctly. The play of children who have very specific interests can sometimes seem repetitive and not as beneficial as high-level play can be. If that is the case, it's important for teachers to consider ways to challenge the children and encourage them to expand their play.

But sometimes these children resist teacher efforts to change what they are doing. So what is a conscientious teacher to do? Rather than forbidding the child's engagement in his all-consuming interest, consider using the child's expertise to bring in other possibilities in his play. Why is this a good teaching strategy? Recognition of a child's expertise can help that child in areas in which he is not strong. Bruce Perry, MD, PhD, tells the story of a young child who becomes fascinated with tadpoles and frogs and learns many aspects of this biological process.

> What is most pleasurable about discovery and mastery is sharing it with someone else? ("Teacher, come look! Tadpoles!").... The teacher smiles, claps, and comments, "You are great. Look at all those tadpoles! You are our science expert!" This rewarding approval causes a surge of pleasure and pride that can sustain the child through new challenges and frustrations.... So later in the day, when this boy is struggling with the introduction of simple math concepts, rather than eroding his esteem by thinking, "I'm stupid, I don't understand," he can think, "I don't get this, but I'm the one who knows about tadpoles." (Perry 2001, 1)

Such affirmation of a child's expertise affects how the child perceives himself in all areas.

Teachers can also use children's all-consuming interests to plan for long-term studies that will allow them to address a number of skills and learning concepts. Two teachers (Erdman and Downing 2015) responded to the interest in superheroes in their program by planning for a number of ways for children to study "The Science of Superheroes." They invited children to

- write stories about how superheroes gained their powers,
- investigate real-life superheroes who help other people,
- explore the science of invisibility and camouflage by investigating butterflies,
- learn more about the super speed of cheetahs,
- look at how fish breathe underwater,
- compare human and bird bone structure to understand why humans can't fly on their own.

The expertise of the children was greatly expanded with very positive results:

> With a more developed understanding of superheroes, the children gained a new vocabulary, and conversations were more complex. The teachers could guide children's superhero play, encourage teamwork, and suggest alternative story lines. Superheroes also became a common play theme for everyone, which led to different friend groups playing together with less friction. (Erdman and Downing 2015, 27)

Reflecting on the Implementation of Individualized Play Plans

No plan is complete without the teacher taking the following steps:

1 Implementing the plan
2 Observing as children engage in the plan
3 Reflecting about what was observed—was the plan successful or unsuccessful?
4 Determining what, if any, changes to make to the original plan

Let's revisit the two completed examples of Individualized Play Planning Sheets that were presented earlier. These completed examples now include the results of the implementation of these plans. Please note that two types of results are addressed: the results for one child and the results for other children.

Individualized Play Planning Sheet

Child's Name: __Henry__   Date: __10-11__   Teacher: __Kristin__

Interests, Favorite Play Areas and Activities That Show the Child's Strengths:	Other Children Who Show Similar Interests and Strengths:
Legos, Blocks, Cars and Trucks	Kevin, Jason, and Oliver

Plans for Play Experiences to Build on the Child's Interests and Strengths:
(What play area, materials, and teacher support strategies will you plan?)

With teacher support, children can count, sort, and build with the various blocks and Legos provided.

Add books about counting and building.

Results of Implementation of Plan:

For this child:
Henry really engaged in our counting and sorting block center. He and Kevin also brought other vehicles to the center.

For the other children:
Kevin, Jason, Oliver, as well as Nadia, Juliette, and Jeremy looked at the counting and building books too and joined in play with blocks.

Individualized Play Planning Sheet

Child's Name: __Alana__   Date: __12/8__   Teacher: __CeCe__

Interests, Favorite Play Areas and Activities That Show the Child's Strengths:	Other Children Who Show Similar Interests and Strengths:
Reading, Writing, Dramatic Area, and Art Zone	Jordyn, Sylvia, Jessica, Devon

Plans for Play Experiences to Build on the Child's Interests and Strengths:
(What play area, materials, and teacher support strategies will you plan?)

Plan to bring more writing materials (crayons, markers, papers) and books to dramatic play.

Set up dramatic play as a restaurant with menus, ordering pads, etc.

Results of Implementation of Plan:

For this child:
Alana and Devon engaged in restaurant play, with Devon being the cook and Alana the customer. We introduced new words: *chef* and *customer*. Alana did the writing for her orders and has visited the writing zone even more frequently.

For the other children:
Jordyn has wanted to write more as well—and does so both in the dramatic area and the writing zone. She writes her name, some of her friends' names, and *love*.

You can also review examples of completed Individualized Play Planning Sheets (with results) in the Developmental Studies in appendix A.

"Sometimes the individualized play planning feels like extra work, but when I planned the activity about Liam's interest, it benefited other children, too." —Jarrod

"This has definitely helped us to think more individually about the children. It seems like whenever we put something in the room that was oriented to one child, more children became interested in it. Then the one for whom it was originally planned stayed there because there were lots of peers with whom she could interact around her interest." —Sue

Conclusion

Teachers observe children's engagement in the play experiences they have planned. They observe as they facilitate the play and also as they sit quietly near the children. Observation is an essential component in gathering information about the success of curriculum planning. Teachers need to be thoughtful and intentional in observing—not always an easy task when they are busily engaged with children throughout the day. Then another task awaits, that of reflecting about what has been observed. Here are some of the reflection questions teachers will want to consider:

- How will you and your colleagues define the success or lack of success of an activity?
- How will you use the information you gathered as you observed the children?
- Will you make changes to the experiences you are offering for all of the children or for a small group of the children?
- Will you need to make adaptations and/or accommodations for individual children to be successful?

Observation and reflection are at the heart of good teaching. In the next chapter, we will explore the importance of observation, time-efficient observation and documentation strategies, and ways that observations can provide assessment information as well as guide curricular planning.

6 Practical Considerations about the Observational Assessment Process

> Learning to be an observer, gathering data about who the children are—their interests, questions, strengths, and challenges—constitutes the starting point for building a child-centered curriculum. Observation is a critical tool for ongoing assessment, planning, and responses to children. (Curtis and Carter 2011, 103)

The process of individualizing curriculum involves teachers observing children in action. As we move forward in creating Developmental Studies for individual children, observing children is an essential part of determining next steps for them. In chapter 1, we identified the five principles underlying the approach to being child-focused and individualizing curriculum. Here is the third foundational principle.

> 3. Assessment is authentic, based on teachers observing in everyday moments and documenting on quick checklists and in descriptive observation notes organized into portfolio collections for each child.
>   It's important for teachers to continue to develop as observers and to effectively use a variety of documentation strategies that are time efficient and do not take away from their presence with the children.

In this chapter, we explore the basics of the observational assessment process. We look at ways to engage in observations that can inform planning by gathering authentic assessment information about each child. We consider some time-efficient observation and documentation strategies and look at the reflection process as an essential part of observing and documenting. Then, in later chapters, various formats for documenting observations will be introduced. (For a more detailed exploration of observation and documentation, see Gronlund and James, *Focused Observations: How to Observe Young Children for Assessment and Curriculum Planning*, Second Edition, 2013).

The Importance of Observation

Teachers observe children all the time. They watch to make sure children are safe. They notice how children react to the different experiences and routines each day in the program. They look to see where and with whom children are playing. They see how children are using materials, expressing their imaginations, and solving problems. They observe to see what children can do independently, where they need assistance, and what is challenging for them.

When a teacher turns her back for a moment to get some materials out of a cupboard, she is still observing—by listening, of course! Observing involves not only using one's eyes but also one's ears to hear the things children are saying and the ways they are communicating with each other. In addition, when a teacher's back is turned, she also has a sixth sense that is engaged—it's as if she has eyes in the back of her head! She notices loud noises and when it is too quiet. Either one might cause her to turn around and observe with her eyes once again. Good teachers are constantly engaged in observation to take care of children and to meet their needs in all areas of development.

Observation is an essential component in the implementation of developmentally appropriate practices. In the third edition of the NAEYC recommendations, the authors tie assessment practices and curriculum planning to teacher observation:

> The excellent teacher uses her observations and other information gathered to inform her planning and teaching, giving careful consideration to the learning experiences needed by the group as a whole and by each individual child. (Copple and Bredekamp 2009, 44)

To identify the learning experiences needed by each child, the teacher gathers information by observing for two purposes:

1   To determine each child's developmental capabilities
2   To determine how the curriculum is meeting each child's needs

Let's consider each of these purposes in more detail.

Observing to Determine Children's Developmental Capabilities

When teachers learn more about a child's development, they are able to plan successful experiences for the child. They will know just how simple or complex an activity should be, what skills the child will need to use, or what assistance and support might benefit the child. They will also observe to determine how to appropriately challenge a child. When a task is too easy, the child is underchallenged and may act out or be uninterested. When it is too hard, he may be overchallenged and again may act out, showing frustration, or feel overwhelmed and discouraged. Teachers use observations not only to meet a child at his developmental level, but also to determine how to help the child move forward in the most beneficial way possible.

Teachers gather information about the whole child, paying attention to multiple domains (or areas of learning) as they observe. In state early learning guidelines, the infant and toddler domains usually include building relationships, language and communication, and physical and motor as well as cognitive development. In state preschool standards, the domains usually include language and literacy, mathematics, scientific thinking, physical and motor and social-emotional development. Your state may have additional ones as well. Teachers look to their state's early learning standards or to accepted developmental reference tools (such as authentic assessment tools approved by their state) to determine what the reasonable expectations are for the age of the child. Then they see where the child is performing in relation to those expectations. This gives them a well-rounded picture of the child's developmental capabilities, areas of strengths, and areas that are challenging for her.

Observing to Determine how the Curriculum is Meeting Each Child's Needs

As a teacher determines a child's developmental capabilities in multiple domains, his next step is to determine how the curriculum is meeting each child's needs. He plans experiences that build on children's strengths and is ready to assist in experiences where the child's capabilities are not as strong. And he observes as he engages with the child in both kinds of experiences. In previous chapters, we considered the importance of observing for children's interests and favorite choices. We saw how these often reflect the strengths of children and how teachers can then plan to build on those in play experiences and playful learning activities. This process will continue as we go beyond interests and favorites and look at observations focused on children's developmental capabilities. In the next chapter, we will learn more about documentation formats for such observations.

The Process of Observing and Documenting

There are practical considerations when teachers observe children. The most common concern expressed by teachers is *time*. But time to do what? How does time become such an important factor in the observation process?

Observation involves focus and memory. Most teachers of young children find that their daily classroom life is full of distractions and interruptions. They may plan to focus on one child or a small group of children. They may set out to gather information about a specific domain or a set of skills. But quickly, in the reality of the classroom, they are interrupted. A child may have tripped and fallen and require attention; two children may be disagreeing about sharing materials and need guidance to resolve their conflict; one child may be wandering the classroom, not engaging productively in any of the experiences available; while another may be trying to protect the construction he has been diligently working on, not wanting any other children to contribute to his efforts. Children will ask questions. They will call for assistance. They will want more playdough available. They will need more paint in the jars at the easel. When teachers are pulled in many different directions, their focus for observation purposes is challenged, and they find that they cannot remember what they observed.

The Importance of Documentation

We know that teachers observe all of the time and that they have an internal videotape running in their heads about which they may reflect at a later time. But that is a lot of information to remember! Not only are teachers monitoring many different things with the children in their classrooms, but they also have busy lives and commitments outside of the classroom. If they rely on their memory alone, they may forget things the children did or miss some aspects of the children's development.

Because of the importance of observation as an assessment process, teachers *cannot* rely solely on their memory when observing. They must document their observations and write them down. They can write brief notes on sticky pads in the moment with children and fill in the details later, or they can write more extensive observations on notebook paper or special observation forms. They can photograph the children in action to give a visual perspective to the written observation. And they can collect samples of the children's creations (such as drawings, paintings, or writing samples) to add evidence to support their written descriptions of what the children did and said.

When teachers describe having issues with time related to observation, they are really describing issues with documentation. Here are some of the most significant questions I hear teachers ask about observation and documentation:

- How can I truly be present with children and still write down all of my observations? If I write while I'm with them, I feel it takes me away from interacting with them.
- Sometimes I get interrupted and don't get back to the documentation in a timely manner, and then I forget what I was trying to document. When is it best to write the documentation?
- What does a good written observation look like? How much should I write?
- How many observations should I document and about what? What are my goals in collecting written documentation of my observations about each child?

Let's provide answers to these questions.

Being Present and in the Moment with Children

This is the all-encompassing, most essential task of teachers of young children. You cannot possibly be a good observer if you are not fully present with the children in your care. And they will not demonstrate as much of what they can do if they do not trust that you are interested, listening, and willing to pay attention and engage with them. Teachers who observe and document do not have to withdraw from the group and sit in a corner writing observation notes—observation and documentation should not take away from good teaching!

So when is it best to document observations? How can a teacher be in the moment with children and still manage to write observation notes? The most successful teachers pick and choose different documentation strategies and formats and use them at different times of the day. Such teachers are always ready to put down their pen and paper and engage fully with the children. If they have a variety of strategies in mind and use them consistently, they are able to create documentation of their observations that helps them know children better and plan appropriately for them throughout the day.

We are going to consider three types of documentation strategies that can all be used while a teacher is engaged with the children. To use them effectively, a teacher will need to be prepared by having the recording methods ready and easily accessed. Plan for a reflection time after the observation. This reflection time is best scheduled when the teacher is not interacting directly with the children. That might be at naptime, while the children are at gym or music, or at the end of the day after the children have left. This reflection time does not need to be long. In fact, five to ten minutes is plenty of time to efficiently document a few observations. Some teachers call this time "Take Five" or "Take Ten" and include their coteachers so that more observations can be discussed and documented. To keep the Take Five meeting brief and productive, focus the conversation on the following questions:

- What did we see the children do or hear them say?
- What happened today that we don't want to forget?

It's important to have a list of the children's names nearby so that no child is overlooked. Many teachers find that having memory joggers to review in this brief meeting reminds them of what the children did throughout the day. Ideas for quickly documenting memory joggers are included in the recommended strategies that follow. Let's look at the three documentation strategies (memory joggers, photos and work samples, and observation formats) and review completed examples of each.

1. Memory joggers. While engaged with the children, write very brief notes that will serve as memory joggers (write on sticky notes, index cards, small pads, adhesive labels, or handheld technological devices); fill out the details of the observation at a later time.

Initial observation: Dylan and Malik—lining up bears, counting 1–10, singing "Ants Go Marching"

Details added at end of day: Today Dylan was lining up the bears. "I'm lining up the army," he said. As he lined them up he sang "The Ants Go Marching," which we learned last week. As he sang, he added bears. He counted correctly with one-to-one correspondence from one to ten but did not maintain one-to-one beyond ten. Malik approached and asked if he could play. Dylan said, "Sure. Do you want to sing?" They continued singing the song as they added bears.

Initial observation: Alissa—alphabet puzzle

Details added at end of day: Today Alissa went to the puzzle shelf and pulled out the ABC puzzle and dumped out all of the letters on the table. I observed as she placed each letter in its place, saying the letter, looking at the picture on the letter piece, and saying the word for that picture (each begins with that letter). She worked at this for approximately ten minutes then called me over to show me what she had done. "I know all my ABCs!" she said.

---

2. Photos and work samples. Take photos or collect work samples while engaged with the children. Review the photo or work sample at a later time and write a description of what the child did and/or said related to that experience (again, you can do this at naptime, during specials, at the end of the day, or during your weekly planning meeting).

Description written at a later time: Samir played with our collection of plastic animals and sorted the ones that live in the ocean by placing them in our "ocean" (a bowl of water). When he finished, he counted how many he had in the water. "I have fifteen!" He did indeed have fifteen sea creatures in his ocean.

Description written at a later time: Today Darla drew a picture of a person and brought it to me. I asked her to sign the various parts of the face and body, but she did not respond. She did point to the marks at the top of the page and signed, "My name."

3. Observation formats. Use a format that allows you to quickly note information about children. You can find blank copies of these three formats in appendix B or download PDF versions from www.redleafpress.org.

Depending on the situation, you can use one of the following:

- Quick Check Recording Sheet
- Brief Notes Recording Sheet
- Small-Group Observation Form

Review the recording sheet at a later time and write a description of what the child did and/or said related to that experience (again, you can do this at naptime, during specials, at the end of the day, or during your weekly planning meeting).

Quick Check Recording Sheet

Children's Names	Date and Activity 12-4 ABC Patterns	Date and Activity	Date and Activity	Date and Activity
Aaron	Yes			
Ashley	No			
Colton	Ab.			
Dylan	Yes			
Gloria	Yes			
Hannah	Yes			
Isaac	Ab.			
Malik	No			
Mason	With help			
Oscar	Yes			
Roberta	With help			
Sofia	Ab.			
Tony	Yes			
Victor	Yes			
Wanda	Yes			
William	No			

Description written at a later time: In the math area, Aaron was invited to work on creating patterns with the colored cubes. After I demonstrated an ABC pattern to him, he began to link orange, blue, and brown cubes he had chosen. When asked to name the pattern he'd created, he did so correctly and continued to link more cubes to extend it.

Brief Notes Recording Sheet

Children's Names	Date and Activity
	Week of Nov. 15 Measurement Activities
Alex	measured with snap cubes, adjusted, counted
Brittany	
Colin	
Dante	compared lengths of blocks
Emily	used measuring tape to measure friends
Frederick	
Gabriel	
Hayley	used measuring tape to measure friends
Kristen	
Michel	compared lengths of blocks
Nico	measured rugs & tables with paper feet
Noelle	
Peter	compared weights of rocks with scale
Samuel	
Stephanie	
Tyler	compared weights of rocks with scale

Description written at a later time: We have been doing a variety of measurement activities in our classroom. Today Alex took a variety of objects to the table to measure with snap cubes. He chose to measure a marker and began to put snap cubes together. His first set of cubes was too long. He then adjusted it to make it just the right length and counted the correct number of cubes he used.

Small-Group Observation Form

Date __10/25__   Activity: __Pumpkin Exploration__

Goal(s): __Sensory Exploration, Vocabulary (seeds, pulp)__

Child's Name: Chelsea	Child's Name: Andrea	Child's Name: Melissa
used whole hand to scoop - took pulp to science area to examine with magnifying glass	scooped with spoon, counted seeds to 12 with 1-1 correspondence	described pulp and seeds as "stinky, wet, and sticky"; joined Chelsea in science area
Child's Name: Courtney	Child's Name: Marie	Child's Name:
Watched scooping without participating	compared inside and outside of pumpkin - "sticky & wet vs. smooth & dry"	
Child's Name:	Child's Name:	Child's Name:
Child's Name:	Child's Name:	Child's Name:

Description written at a later time: We have been learning about the life cycle of a pumpkin and had previously looked closely at the outer part of our class pumpkin. Today in small group, we cut it open and explored with scooping spoons. Chelsea and the other girls in the group worked cooperatively, talking about what to do. "Let's take the top off," Chelsea suggested. "Eeww, it stinks! Can we take the stuff out? What should we do with it?" The group decided to scoop out the seeds and pulp into a bowl. As others used their spoons, Chelsea put her whole hand inside the pumpkin and began pulling out the pulp. "I did this at home with our pumpkin!" Then she asked me, "Can we put some of this pulp in the science center?" We did so and Chelsea used the magnifying glass to look more closely at the pulp and seeds for approximately five minutes.

As teachers try out these different documentation strategies and begin the daily practice of a Take Five reflection meeting, they will want to consider which methods worked best for which situations. Each teacher needs to figure out the ways that she can be most successful at documenting the observations she wants to remember. That involves trial and error in order to determine what is best for each individual. Teachers may learn their colleagues prefer different methods than they do—that is not a problem as long as everyone is committed to collecting documentation that will help them know children better.

Writing a Good Observation

A good observation is not necessarily very long. It is factual and descriptive and provides details about what a child can do. It is focused and clear and provides information specific to the child and who he is. Let's explore the aspects of good observations.

First, a good observation is a factual description. When documenting observations, teachers are gathering information. They are conducting their research about children. They are like detectives who are pulling together evidence in order to solve a puzzle. In this case, the puzzle is the child. Who is she? What can she do? Where does she need assistance? Therefore, written observations need to be factual and descriptive rather than judgmental or interpretive. They include only what the child did and/or said. They do not include the teacher's opinion or evaluation of the child.

Writing only the facts of an observation can be challenging for some teachers. They know their children well and certainly do have opinions about the child's strengths and areas of challenge. Therefore, as they write descriptions of what they have seen the child do, they need an internal editor reminding them to focus on what actually was observed.

Here is a chart that can help with that internal editing process. By no means is this chart inclusive of every possible word and phrase to avoid or use. However, it can be a helpful reminder. Many teachers print it out and keep it nearby as they document observations so that they can stick to the facts in their descriptions of the children's actions. You can find a copy of this chart in appendix B or download a PDF version from www.redleafpress.org.

Words and Phrases to Avoid	Words and Phrases to Use
The child loves . . .	He often chooses . . .
The child likes . . .	I saw him . . .
He enjoys . . .	I heard her say . . .
She spends a long time at . . .	He spends five minutes doing . . .
It seems like . . .	She said . . .
It appears . . .	Almost every day, he . . .
I thought . . .	Once or twice a month, she . . .
I felt . . .	Each time, he . . .
I wonder . . .	She consistently . . .
He does . . . very well . . .	We observed a pattern of . . .
She is bad at . . .	
This is difficult for . . .	

Where does evaluation fit in, then? There is no question that teachers need to evaluate children's progress. However, evaluation is not part of the process when collecting information and documenting observations. The information is interpreted and evaluated *after* it is documented. We will consider when a teacher does evaluate and interpret in later chapters.

"I tried to write 'I saw' and 'I heard.' It was hard at times. Now I have been referring to the charts and believe that I am writing in an objective way." —Kristin

To write factually and descriptively involves self-reflection. When documenting observations, it's important for teachers to consider their own assumptions and biases about children. There is no question that teaching young children can be challenging—they have lots of energy and enthusiasm; they are keenly interested in everything around them; they are not quiet; they want to run and jump and play; they do not always know how to express their feelings through words rather than actions. However, teachers' observations should not be influenced by any frustrations they might be feeling. Instead, effective teachers take time to pause and reflect so that they can open their hearts and minds to who the children truly are. Curtis and Carter (2011) suggest that teachers ask themselves, "What child do you see?" and use the following strategies to help them remain open and ready for observing children without assumptions and biases:

- Meet up with children's hearts and minds, not their behaviors.
- Recognize children's eagerness for relationships.
- Notice and marvel at children's positive interactions with each other.
- Coach children to offer their ideas and competence.
- Reinforce children's positive social interactions. (84–88)

What else might you add?

As you review the observation examples throughout this book, note that they are objective and descriptive. In the sample Developmental Studies in appendix A, you will see that the documented observations provide factual evidence to help the teacher plan more effectively for the child.

How Much to Document in One Observation

Another concern about observation and documentation that teachers raise is uncertainty about how much information to include. If teachers try to write everything down that they see children doing, they will not have time to do anything else! Therefore, they need to set goals for their observations and make choices about what and how much to document. The best documentation is often brief, focused, and to the point. It is not necessary to write a running record of everything a child does and/or says in a set period of time.

"I had to learn not to write a running record and not stress about it. Photos were helpful to add more information to my brief written descriptions." —Jordan

Two to four sentences or phrases describing the child's actions, engagement, and/or interactions can be very informative when teachers make sure they do the following:

- Indicate the purpose of the observation.
- Include the necessary details to meet the proposed purpose.
- Check that the unique characteristics and capabilities of the child being observed shine through in the documentation.

Here are two examples of documented observations to consider. Can you determine the purpose? What details led you to that conclusion? What did you learn about each of the children?

During choice time, Emily used both sign and her voice to organize a group to use playdough at the sensory table. She divided the playdough and reminded the group to share. The play became interactive, with an in-depth conversation about the zoo, and lasted for twenty-five minutes.

Purpose: To capture Emily's ability to socialize and communicate with others
Details: Descriptions of Emily's actions and the results
Individuality: Shows Emily's initiation and leadership in forming a group of peers

I invited children to create pictures of things they can see in the sky and gave them chart paper with two columns labeled "Day" and "Night." Jackson got index cards for himself and the four other children so they could draw pictures and place them on the chart. At one point, the cards fell on the floor and Jackson picked them up. There was a discussion about where to put a drawing of an airplane and Jackson said, "Airplanes can fly at both day and night so maybe we can put it in the middle." All agreed.

Purpose: To capture Jackson's use of language in conversation with other children
Details: Direct quotes and description of the situation
Individuality: Jackson's helpfulness and problem solving about where to place the airplane

What are some purposes for observations? Generally teachers focus their observations on what children are showing they can do in various domains. If a teacher is trying to write down how a child uses his fine-motor skills, then she will want to include details about his use of his hands and fingers to manipulate small objects or writing or drawing tools. And she will pay attention to his hand-eye coordination as he works with materials. If a teacher is trying to show a child's progress in mathematical problem solving, she will want to include a history of what the child has done when figuring out quantities or spatial relationships and then relate that to the current observation. Because of the identified focus, the teacher knows that she does not have to include every single thing the child does or says. Instead, she edits herself as she writes, asking, "What are the essential things to include related to the purpose of this observation?"

It's important to include details that are unique to the child. While some observational assessment tools include items to be checked off on a list of developmental skills and competencies, they also include written descriptions of children at work and play. For our Developmental Studies, we will emphasize these descriptions. To truly individualize curriculum, a teacher must record the different ways that each child goes about figuring things out, communicating with others, making friendships, and acquiring skills. No two children are exactly alike, and their differences should shine through in written observations of them in action.

Organizing a Set of Observations

Teachers often ask the questions, "How many observations should I document and about what?" "What are my goals in collecting written documentation of my observations about each child?" For the purposes of our Developmental Studies, we will gather observations that cover *all* of the domains of development. These domains may be defined in a state's early learning standards or in the authentic assessment tool that a program has adopted. Usually five to seven domains are identified in these documents. As I stated earlier, at minimum, the infant and toddler domains usually include building relationships, language and communication, physical and motor as well as cognitive development. The preschool domains usually include language and literacy, mathematics, scientific thinking, physical and motor and social emotional-development.

Because observations are meant to provide evidence of children's development across time, a minimum of two sets should be documented. Some programs target the collection of one set of observations in the fall and the second in the winter/spring. Some identify three collection periods (fall, winter, and spring). In either case, the observations can be planned for related domains. Then they can be compared across time to show the child's progress in that domain.

So the simple answer to the question, how many observations should be documented per child? Four to seven related to the domains of early learning standards or assessment tools, two to three times per year.

An important consideration when documenting observations across time is to focus not only on the domains but also the indicators or benchmarks within the domain. To see how the child progresses, the documentation should relate to similar aspects of development. Tracking a child's progress in his expressive language will require that the teacher observe and document conversations that include direct quotes from the child. Tracking a child's progress in playing cooperatively with others will necessitate written descriptions of the child playing with other children. In the next chapter, we will explore how to document observations in a portfolio format that will guide you in capturing children's progress in various domains across time.

Conclusion

Observational assessment can be an all-encompassing process that requires teachers to determine their documentation strategies, organize the necessary materials, and focus their observations. But what do teachers do with their completed documentation? They use their observations to determine how to better meet the needs of each child—that is the most critical step in individualizing curriculum! Documented observations provide information you can use to plan for play experiences and learning activities that will meet each child where she is at and help her to move forward. You will learn what she can do on her own and where she needs assistance. Your observations can give you the confidence and certainty that you are being the best teacher you can be! The remaining chapters will show you ways to make the connections between your observations and your curricular planning.

> "Based on my portfolio documentation for Thomas, I will build a lesson plan based on his interests that would include the whole group. We'll encourage children to use large connecting blocks to construct a scene, talk about it, offer books related to it, and relate it to their gross-motor development, language, and creativity." —Kristin

Rich, Informative Portfolio Documentation

Teachers observe their children all the time and document some of those observations. To strengthen a child-focused, individualized approach to teaching, let's look at how to organize those documented observations into portfolios for each child. We will use a documentation format that allows the teacher to relate her description of what the child said and did to the domains the child demonstrated as well as to specific benchmarks or indicators the child is working toward.

Why Use a Portfolio Format?

Teachers identify organization as one of the biggest issues they have when it comes to observation and documentation. Many feel overwhelmed by the documentation they have collected. They may have multiple sticky notes where they briefly jotted down what children did or said or have checklists where they noted what children showed they could do. They may feel unsure about the steps they need to take to

- pull all of their notes together in a meaningful format,
- present the information they have gained from these observations to the children's families, and
- effectively review and reflect on the observations to plan curriculum that meets the needs of each child.

The portfolio format becomes a way for teachers to do all of these tasks by organizing documentation.

Teachers often report that families love portfolios. When well organized and clearly linked to learning goals, portfolios help families see their children in action. As they read the teacher's descriptions of their children, they feel the teacher has provided a window into the classroom day through which they can learn more about what their children do and how they interact with other children and with their teachers. They enjoy seeing photographs of their children and reading stories about them. Many families treasure their children's portfolios and thank the teacher profusely for giving them this evidence of their children's growth and progress over time. And many teachers report that after reviewing the portfolios with them, families better understand the learning that occurs as children play and the ways teachers facilitate that learning and address standards and expectations. Sharing portfolios with families creates a win-win situation for everyone!

> "I shared the portfolio observations with the families, and they were thrilled with them!" —Kelly

> "I did use the portfolios and photos in my IEP meetings, and parents were genuinely excited to see what their child had done." —Cathy

The Portfolio Forms

The documentation format we will use was originally designed for the book *Focused Portfolios: A Complete Assessment for the Young Child* (Gronlund and Engel 2001) and has been adapted and reformatted over the years (Gronlund 2013). You can find a copy of this form in appendix B or download a PDF version from www.redleafpress.org.

Portfolio Collection Form

Child's Name: _____   Date: _____   Observer: _____

Domain(s): _____

Learning goal(s) demonstrated in this documentation: _____

_____

_____

Check off whatever applies to the context of this observation:

☐ child-initiated activity   ☐ done independently   ☐ time spent (1 to 5 minutes)

☐ teacher-initiated activity   ☐ done with adult guidance ☐ time spent (5 to 15 minutes)

☐ new task for this child   ☐ done with peer(s)   ☐ time spent (more than 15 minutes)

☐ familiar task for this child

Anecdotal note: Describe what you saw the child do and/or heard the child say (attach a photo or work sample if appropriate).

You can see that the format includes places for the teacher to write various kinds of information at the top of the page and to document the description of what the child did and/or said at the bottom. In addition, a photograph can be inserted next to the observation, or a child's work sample can be attached on a separate page. The information at the top is filled in *after* the observation has taken place. It includes the child's name, the date of the observation, the observer's name, and the domains and the learning goals (indicators or benchmarks within the identified domains) demonstrated in the observation. There is also a context box in which the teacher checks off any of the aspects of the child's actions that apply. Teachers report that this checklist of contextual information is a real time-saver and helps limit their written descriptions so that they are brief, focused, and to the point.

Here are two examples of completed portfolio forms for different children. You may want to read through the observation description first, then read the information at the top. Do you see evidence of the domains and learning goals demonstrated in the child's actions and/or words documented in the description? A clear connection should exist between the two.

Portfolio Collection Form

Child's Name: Hayley   Date: 12/5   Observer: Kristin

Domain(s): Approaches to Learning, Social/Emotional

Learning goal(s) demonstrated in this documentation: _____

concentrate on a task, complete a sequence, use of imagination, role-playing adult roles

Check off whatever applies to the context of this observation:

☑ child-initiated activity   ☑ done independently   ☐ time spent (1 to 5 minutes)

☐ teacher-initiated activity   ☐ done with adult guidance   ☑ time spent (5 to 15 minutes)

☐ new task for this child   ☐ done with peer(s)

☑ familiar task for this child   ☐ time spent (more than 15 minutes)

Anecdotal note: Describe what you saw the child do and/or heard the child say (attach a photo or work sample if appropriate).

Hayley consistently chooses to play with the dolls and play strollers in the gym and outside. Today I saw her choose a baby and then look through the doll clothes. She chose a blanket and placed the baby in the stroller and covered her up. Hayley then spent about six minutes pushing her baby around in the stroller.

See photo.

Portfolio Collection Form

Child's Name: Denise   Date: 11/4   Observer: Jordan

Domain(s): Cognitive, Language

Learning goal(s) demonstrated in this documentation: _____

Creative play, sorting and categorizing, expressive language and use of vocabulary

Check off whatever applies to the context of this observation:

☐ child-initiated activity   ☑ done independently   ☐ time spent (1 to 5 minutes)

☑ teacher-initiated activity   ☐ done with adult guidance   ☑ time spent (5 to 15 minutes)

☐ new task for this child   ☑ done with peer(s)

☑ familiar task for this child   ☐ time spent (more than 15 minutes)

Anecdotal note: Describe what you saw the child do and/or heard the child say (attach a photo or work sample if appropriate).

Denise was lining up ocean animals on a tray. She told her friends sitting with her that she went to the aquarium and saw people swimming with the fish. Then she said, "I'm a teacher about animals. I saw octopus like this (she held up a starfish) and the penguins are outside."

There should be a set time period in which teachers are building portfolios for the children. There can be a fall collection period (from September to December or limited to only October and November). Then there can be a winter/spring collection period (from February to April or maybe limited to only March and April). If three collection periods are determined to be most appropriate, they might occur as follows:

- Fall (September–November)
- Winter (January–February)
- Spring (March–May)

The scheduling of family/teacher conferences may influence the timing of portfolio collection as may the program calendar (such as the dates of holiday vacations). To compare observations and determine children's progress at least two collection periods must be planned.

Authentic Portfolio Collection

All of the observation strategies that I discussed in the previous chapter can be used for portfolio collection. Teachers are not expected to set up "portfolio collection days" or "portfolio activities." Rather, they are to continue to observe children throughout the day, in all sorts of experiences and activities, and then to document some of their observations. This is authentic rather than on-demand assessment. The teacher is capturing examples of children's learning and progress in everyday experiences in the classroom instead of calling children over to a special one-on-one or small-group task.

Let's think back to the play plan based on children's interests referred to in chapter 5. As a teacher implements that plan with various children, he has a perfect opportunity to observe children engaged in an authentic experience. If he documents what the children did and said while they played related to their interests, he can use some of that documentation in the children's portfolios. Here is an example taken from the play plan about Alana. The teacher's observation and description of the results of her play experience can easily be transferred to the portfolio format with additional information added about domains, learning goals, and the context of Alana's involvement.

Individualized Play Planning Sheet

Child's Name: __Alana__   Date: __12/8__   Teacher: __CeCe__

Interests, Favorite Play Areas and Activities That Show the Child's Strengths:	Other Children Who Show Similar Interests and Strengths:
Reading, Writing, Dramatic Area, and Art Zone	Jordyn, Sylvia, Jessica, Devon

Plans for Play Experiences to Build on the Child's Interests and Strengths:
(What play area, materials, and teacher support strategies will you plan?)

Plan to bring more writing materials (crayons, markers, papers) and books to dramatic play.

Set up dramatic play as a restaurant with menus, ordering pads, etc.

Results of Implementation of Plan:

For this child:
Alana and Devon engaged in restaurant play, with Devon being the cook and Alana the customer. We introduced new words: *chef* and *customer*. Alana did the writing for her orders and has visited the writing zone even more frequently.

For the other children:
Jordyn has wanted to write more as well—and does so both in the dramatic area and the writing zone. She writes her name, some of her friends' names, and *love*.

Portfolio Collection Form

Child's Name: __Alana__   Date: __12/15__   Observer: __CeCe__

Domain(s): __Cognitive, Language, Social/Emotional, Literacy__

Learning goal(s) demonstrated in this documentation: _____

__Role playing, using new vocabulary, playing with a peer, using emergent writing for__

__various purposes__

Check off whatever applies to the context of this observation:

- ☐ child-initiated activity
- ☑ teacher-initiated activity
- ☑ new task for this child
- ☐ familiar task for this child

- ☐ done independently
- ☐ done with adult guidance
- ☑ done with peer(s)

- ☐ time spent (1 to 5 minutes)
- ☐ time spent (5 to 15 minutes)
- ☑ time spent (more than 15 minutes)

Anecdotal note: Describe what you saw the child do and/or heard the child say (attach a photo or work sample if appropriate).

Over several days, Alana and Devon engaged in restaurant play, with Devon being the cook and Alana the customer. We introduced new words, "chef" and "customer," which they used in their play. Alana did the writing for her orders, making letter-like shapes, some recognizable letters, and scribble writing. Other children joined in as well to help cook or to order food.

Planning and intentionality on the part of the teacher is needed so that the complete collection of documentation in the portfolio does the following three things:

1   Addresses each of the domains identified in the observational assessment process (taken from early learning standards or authentic assessment tools)
2   Shows evidence of specific learning goals, benchmarks, or indicators that can be tracked across time for progress
3   Shows the unique ways that the child demonstrated her capabilities

Young children do not demonstrate their capabilities related to only one discrete skill or even one domain. Teachers report that they can identify multiple domains when reviewing their observations and determining what the children demonstrated. In this way, teachers are creating a rich collection of observations that show many skills and capabilities for each child without having to complete more than four to seven portfolio forms. What many teachers do, then, is organize children's portfolios so that they identify a primary domain on each form. Other domains are identified as well (with goals, benchmarks, or indicators included) but are considered as complementary. Teachers label a file folder with each child's name and place the portfolio forms in the folder as they complete them. Each child's folder then will contain four to seven portfolio forms from each collection period (whether that is fall and spring or fall, winter, and spring).

> "I found it so helpful that you can use one portfolio sample to discuss and document more than one domain and standard." —Danielle

You can review the portfolio collections in the two complete Developmental Studies in appendix A to see how the teachers organized their observations by domains and identified one as the primary focus for each of the portfolio forms.

Domains are broad categories of development and include many learning goals, indicators, or benchmarks. For example, the domain of language and literacy in the preschool years encompasses speaking, listening, emergent reading, and emergent writing. And there are many more specific learning goals within each of those areas. For example, speaking includes articulation, communicating wants and needs, use of sentence structure, and expanding vocabulary. That is why both the domains and the learning goals are identified on the portfolio forms. By relating specific early learning standards or indicators from an assessment tool to the observation, teachers are more able to track children's progress across time. When they are not as specific, it is difficult to compare a later observation with an earlier one and draw conclusions about how the child is growing.

Here are examples of portfolio forms (one from the fall and one from spring) that contain observations of the same child. As you read through the information on the forms, consider the following questions:

- Can you determine whether the child is progressing in her capabilities or not?
- What evidence do you have (or is missing) to come to that conclusion?

Portfolio Collection Form

Child's Name: Caroline   Date: 10/31   Observer: Sara

Domain(s): Cognitive (Math): Patterns, Functions, Algebra; Approaches to Learning

Learning goal(s) demonstrated in this documentation:

identifies, copies, extends, and creates simple patterns in daily activities and play;

developing independence and showing initiative

Check off whatever applies to the context of this observation:

- ☑ child-initiated activity
- ☑ teacher-initiated activity
- ☑ new task for this child
- ☐ familiar task for this child
- ☑ done independently
- ☐ done with adult guidance
- ☐ done with peer(s)
- ☐ time spent (1 to 5 minutes)
- ☑ time spent (5 to 15 minutes)
- ☐ time spent (more than 15 minutes)

Anecdotal note: Describe what you saw the child do and/or heard the child say (attach a photo or work sample if appropriate).

Our class has been studying ABC patterns and creating them in many different ways. Today Caroline created an ABC pattern using foam sticker leaves. She independently continued the pattern until her strip of paper was full. She made one error in her pattern. When I brought it to her attention, she said, "Whoops!" and corrected it without any needed guidance. She read the pattern aloud when she was done.

Portfolio Collection Form

Child's Name: Caroline   Date: 4/24   Observer: Sara

Domain(s): Cognitive (Math): Number Sense & Operations; Approaches to Learning

Learning goal(s) demonstrated in this documentation:

Uses one-to-one correspondence when counting; identifies and names numerals;

solves problems involving quantities; shows eagerness and curiosity as a learner

Check off whatever applies to the context of this observation:

- ☑ child-initiated activity
- ☐ teacher-initiated activity
- ☐ new task for this child
- ☑ familiar task for this child
- ☐ done independently
- ☐ done with adult guidance
- ☑ done with peer(s)
- ☐ time spent (1 to 5 minutes)
- ☐ time spent (5 to 15 minutes)
- ☑ time spent (more than 15 minutes)

Anecdotal note: Describe what you saw the child do and/or heard the child say (attach a photo or work sample if appropriate).

Caroline chose to work at the writing center on an optional math learning experience. She chose a "dog" from our "pet shop" and proceeded to make food for the dog. She sat for about 15 minutes creating "food" for the dog. I asked her if she could give her dog 3 bones, which she did successfully. Next I suggested 7 bones—and again she counted out successfully, touching each bone as she counted. We went on until she had fed the dog between 1 and 10 bones. To stretch the activity, I asked her what would happen if a dog took a bone away from her dog. She told me correctly the amount with one less and one more.

You can see that these two observations are about the child's understanding of math; however, the specific goals or benchmarks do not document the child's progress over time. One cannot compare patterning to counting. They are different skills. When a teacher wants to collect evidence that will document progress, she needs to consider what aspect of the domain she noted in the earlier observation and follow that same aspect in later observations. To do this effectively, she needs to think about the learning goals for which it is most important to track progress.

"I realized I was not focusing on choosing standards that showed growth across time. This was a big revelation. In the future, I'm going to give more thought about what standards will be best to follow across the year." —Kelly

"Keeping it to similar benchmarks in a domain from fall to spring was an effective strategy. It helped me build a better case from point A to point B." —Sara

When tracking children's progress, it's best to choose learning goals that are broader in scope and relate more to the overall development of a child in a domain rather than ones that are isolated skills. Let's consider some learning goals that are easily tracked for progress and contrast them with ones that are not.

Broader Learning Goals to Track in a Portfolio

- children's use of language to communicate with others
- children's interest and enjoyment of books and reading experiences
- children's emergent writing
- children's understanding of quantities as demonstrated in mathematical problem solving (not just counting)
- children's understanding of geometry and spatial relationships (not just naming shapes)
- children's understanding of measurement with nonstandard and/or standard measurement tools
- children's scientific understanding related to hypothesizing and experimenting
- children's knowledge of their community as demonstrated in dramatic play

Limited Learning Goals Best Documented on a Checklist

- the number of steps a child can follow in an auditory direction from a teacher
- the number of letters and/or sounds a child can identify or write
- the numerals or shape names a child can identify
- the amount to which a child counts with one-to-one correspondence
- fine-motor skills, such as pincer grasp and scissor skills
- gross-motor skills, such as hopping on one foot, galloping, or skipping

Here are examples of portfolio forms (one from fall and one from spring) that contain observations of the same child. As you read through the information on the forms, note how clearly the broadness of the learning goals helps the documentation show the child's progress across time.

Portfolio Collection Form

Child's Name: Joe   Date: 11/1   Observer: Kelly

Domain(s): Language and Literacy, Approaches to Learning

Learning goal(s) demonstrated in this documentation:

Beginning letter recognition; shows eagerness and curiosity as a learner

Check off whatever applies to the context of this observation:

- ☑ child-initiated activity
- ☐ teacher-initiated activity
- ☑ new task for this child
- ☑ familiar task for this child

- ☑ done independently
- ☐ done with adult guidance
- ☐ done with peer(s)

- ☐ time spent (1 to 5 minutes)
- ☑ time spent (5 to 15 minutes)
- ☐ time spent (more than 15 minutes)

Anecdotal note: Describe what you saw the child do and/or heard the child say (attach a photo or work sample if appropriate).

Today Joe chose to work with the magnetic alphabet letters and numerals on the white board. He arranged them left to right in rows and identified the letters A, B, C, and X. He also named the numbers 4 and 7. Then he took them all off and announced, "I'm going to make Joe." He searched through the letters until he found the correct ones and called out, "I did it!"

See 2 photos.

Portfolio Collection Form

Child's Name: Joe   Date: 5/8   Observer: Kelly

Domain(s): Language and Literacy: Writing; Approaches to Learning

Learning goal(s) demonstrated in this documentation:

Uses early forms of writing to inform or communicate; prints letter-like symbols, letters or representations; shows initiative; focuses on a task

Check off whatever applies to the context of this observation:

- ☑ child-initiated activity
- ☐ teacher-initiated activity
- ☐ new task for this child
- ☑ familiar task for this child

- ☑ done independently
- ☑ done with adult guidance
- ☑ done with peer(s)

- ☐ time spent (1 to 5 minutes)
- ☐ time spent (5 to 15 minutes)
- ☑ time spent (more than 15 minutes)

Anecdotal note: Describe what you saw the child do and/or heard the child say (attach a photo or work sample if appropriate).

Joe chose the writing center and pulled out his name card. He wrote his name with ease three times, saying the letters aloud each time he wrote them.

Joe signs his name on his drawings and artworks, signs in at our "Good Morning" book every morning, and names many other letters correctly, especially if they are in his friends' names, such as Grady and Josh.

See photo.

You can review the portfolio collections in the two complete Developmental Studies in appendix A to see what learning goals the teachers documented across time to show how the children were progressing in their skills and capabilities.

Documentation That Reflects the Uniqueness of Each Child

No two children's portfolio collections should look the same. Each child is unique in the ways that he shows what he knows and can do. Children may participate in the same experiences and activities, but their interactions with the materials and with others will be different. These differences should shine through in the teacher's written descriptions. When documentation is individualized in this way, both teachers and families see the children's personalities, strengths, interests, and learning approaches clearly represented on the page. Here are two examples of portfolio documentation that show the children's unique ways of demonstrating what they can do.

Portfolio Collection Form

Child's Name: Devon   Date: 11/5   Observer: Danielle

Domain(s): Cognition and General Knowledge: Math (geometry) and Social Studies

Learning goal(s) demonstrated in this documentation:

Recognize and create geometric shapes; with modeling & support, negotiate to solve

social conflicts with peers

Check off whatever applies to the context of this observation:

☑ child-initiated activity   ☐ done independently   ☐ time spent (1 to 5 minutes)
☐ teacher-initiated activity   ☑ done with adult guidance ☑ time spent (5 to 15 minutes)
☑ new task for this child   ☐ done with peer(s)
☐ familiar task for this child   ☐ time spent (more than 15 minutes)

Anecdotal note: Describe what you saw the child do and/or heard the child say (attach a photo or work sample if appropriate).

Devon played with a set of materials that included big lines, little lines, big curves, and little curves. As he moved the shapes around, he figured out that two big curves placed together forms a circle. "Look!" he called out. "I made a circle!" I asked him what he could turn the circle into. "A face—but I don't have any eyes." He looked over at a friend and told me, "They have all of the shapes." I asked him what he could do about that, and he replied, "Use my words." He walked over to a peer and asked, "Can I have some shapes?" The peer replied, "No." I prompted him to ask his peer to share the shapes. The child thought for a moment, then asked Devon to show him how to make a circle. The two worked together to make several people.

See photo.

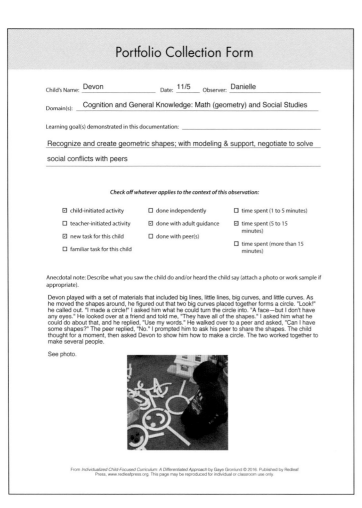

Portfolio Collection Form

Child's Name: Noah   Date: 9/24   Observer: Cathy

Domain(s): Cognition and General Knowledge: Science; Language; Fine Motor

Learning goal(s) demonstrated in this documentation:

Use observation skills of living things; communicate with others; use writing and

drawing tools; use correct grasp when writing and drawing

Check off whatever applies to the context of this observation:

☑ child-initiated activity   ☑ done independently   ☐ time spent (1 to 5 minutes)
☐ teacher-initiated activity   ☐ done with adult guidance ☑ time spent (5 to 15 minutes)
☑ new task for this child   ☐ done with peer(s)
☐ familiar task for this child   ☐ time spent (more than 15 minutes)

Anecdotal note: Describe what you saw the child do and/or heard the child say (attach a photo or work sample if appropriate).

Our class has added a new pet—a classroom frog. Noah kept signing "frog" to everyone who came into the room. He got some paper and pencil and stood by the back counter, looking at the frog and drawing him in his home.

See work sample.

There is nothing wrong with teachers writing a description of an experience or activity and duplicating that description on several children's portfolio forms. However, the description does not end there. They also add information about how each child went about engaging in the experience or activity. That will be where the differences are evident. Here are examples of portfolio documentation showing how two children participated in the same experience but in unique ways.

Portfolio Collection Form

Child's Name: Zane   Date: 10/29   Observer: Kelly

Domain(s): Cognitive: Math; Social/Emotional; Approaches to Learning

Learning goal(s) demonstrated in this documentation: _____

Describe and compare measurable attributes; work cooperatively with peers;

problem-solve

Check off whatever applies to the context of this observation:

☐ child-initiated activity   ☐ done independently   ☐ time spent (1 to 5 minutes)
☒ teacher-initiated activity   ☒ done with adult guidance   ☒ time spent (5 to 15 minutes)
☒ new task for this child   ☒ done with peer(s)
☐ familiar task for this child   ☐ time spent (more than 15 minutes)

Anecdotal note: Describe what you saw the child do and/or heard the child say (attach a photo or work sample if appropriate).

In small group, I introduced the activity of measuring each other using paper pumpkin cutouts. The children discussed ways to do so and decided that the person being measured would lay down on the floor and the one measuring would line up the pumpkins next to him or her. We practiced in small group and then the materials were made available during Choice Time. Zane and Anton chose to measure each other.

As Anton lay on the floor, Zane placed the pumpkins next to him with varying gaps between the pumpkins. I discussed with both boys about the need for accuracy in measurement. Zane did not make any adjustments to the pumpkins and counted them as they lay—7 pumpkins. We recorded his count. Then, compared it to Anton's measurement of Zane (13). The boys stood back to back and determined they are the same height—but their counted pumpkins were very different. Zane measured Anton a second time, and this time moved the pumpkins right next to each other and got a more accurate measurement of 13.

See photo.

Portfolio Collection Form

Child's Name: Anton   Date: 10/29   Observer: Kelly

Domain(s): Cognitive: Math; Social/Emotional; Approaches to Learning

Learning goal(s) demonstrated in this documentation: _____

Describe and compare measurable attributes; work cooperatively with peers;

problem-solve

Check off whatever applies to the context of this observation:

☐ child-initiated activity   ☐ done independently   ☐ time spent (1 to 5 minutes)
☒ teacher-initiated activity   ☒ done with adult guidance   ☒ time spent (5 to 15 minutes)
☒ new task for this child   ☒ done with peer(s)
☐ familiar task for this child   ☐ time spent (more than 15 minutes)

Anecdotal note: Describe what you saw the child do and/or heard the child say (attach a photo or work sample if appropriate).

In small group, I introduced the activity of measuring each other using paper pumpkin cutouts. The children discussed ways to do so and decided that the person being measured would lay down on the floor and the one measuring would line up the pumpkins next to him or her. We practiced in small group and then the materials were made available during Choice Time. Zane and Anton chose to measure each other.

First, Zane measured Anton (with a result of 7 pumpkins). Then Anton measured Zane, carefully placing the pumpkins right next to each other so that the stem touched the bottom of the next pumpkin. His result was 13 (which he counted with 1-1 correspondence). Anton called me over and said, "Ms. Kelly, can you help us see if we're both the same?" I suggested that the boys stand back-to-back and determined they are the same height. Anton told Zane, "You gotta do it again, Zane. Make sure the pumpkins are touching each other so we're the same."

Practical Considerations for Portfolio Collection

Portfolios based on observations require that teachers plan for the collection process. Here are some of the steps that need to be taken before beginning the collection:

1   With colleagues (other teachers, director, principal), teachers determine the primary domains for which they will document observations.
2   With colleagues, teachers determine how many times across the year they will complete portfolio forms (a minimum of two times is necessary to show progress).

3   Teachers may want to identify the broader goals in the benchmarks or indicators of their early learning standards or observational assessment tool to compare to show progress.

Once these tasks have been completed, teachers begin observing children and documenting some of what they observe. Because they know the domains (and maybe the learning goals) they want to document, teachers are ready to capture descriptions and photos related to those. They can plan experiences and activities that lead children to engage in ways that will give teachers specific information related to specific domains. This may take some experimentation and discussion. Teachers can invite their colleagues to try different ways of planning for portfolio collection and then determine what works best for each person.

Conclusion

The portfolio collections are not just folders of paperwork to be set aside. Nor are they only a family communication tool. They are meant to help teachers assess where children are in their development. Teachers can then plan curriculum that will meet each child where she is successful and help her to move forward in acquiring skills and knowledge. The portfolios are meant to be studied, referred to, and reflected on as teachers consider what they are learning about each child that will make their curricular planning more relevant to each child's needs.

In the next chapter, we will look at the reflection process in more depth and provide a tool for teachers to use in their review of children's portfolios for the purpose of planning individualized curricular strategies.

> "I have a clear picture of what my portfolio collection should look like. I like this format because I can reflect and really see growth. In the future, I will plan to better identify what my portfolio goals should be and plan more intentionally for them." —Kelly

Engaging in Deep Reflection about Children

As we have said throughout this book, teachers are very busy people. They are always "on call" in the classroom. They are constantly multitasking as they keep children safe, appropriately stimulated, and emotionally supported. As they go through the day, they are pulled in multiple directions, continually changing "hats" to play the role that is needed at the time. They may be acting in any of these roles:

- instructor
- facilitator
- materials provider
- furniture arranger
- song leader
- storyteller
- observer and documenter
- nose and tear wiper
- bathroom monitor
- cleaning lady
- snack organizer
- hugger and back rubber
- reminder
- family supporter

The list can go on and on, can't it? What else would you add?

Yet one of the most important tasks a teacher must engage in is reflection and planning. These two processes are essential to truly facilitate and support children's development and success. There is no question that teachers engage in spontaneous reflection in the classroom and make adjustments in their planning on the fly. They must be flexible, constantly observing to determine how things are going each minute of the day, and changing what needs changing in the moment. This is the "on call" part of teaching.

But teachers cannot rely only on planning in the spur of the moment. They must also plan intentionally, outside of their time with the children. They need to pause and think about the day or the week, and to consider what worked for individual children and for the group. But planning time is not done in isolation. In the best-case scenario, teachers engage in conversation with their teaching team to gain different perspectives about what was successful and what was not. They review the videotapes running in their heads, replaying what occurred in various situations and planned experiences. And they review their documented observations (in the portfolios and elsewhere) to plan what they will change in the environment and in the experiences they offer, what will remain the same, and what individual adaptations might be needed to help different children. True planning time involves reflection about observations. The observations then lead teachers to plan the most effective curricular strategies.

> "In planning, I was more thoughtful. Instead of just planning for the whole group, I was really thinking about how my lessons were going to affect each child." —Kelly

> "When we take the time to reflect and discuss individual children, I find it really helpful in making specific plans." —Jarrod

This means dedicating time away from the children for reflection and planning. Some programs provide paid weekly planning time (one-half to one hour) for teachers, but others expect this planning to occur after the workday is over. While that may not seem fair or appropriate, planning is an essential part of being an effective teacher and cannot be neglected. Young children need dedicated professionals who will commit to taking time once a week to intentionally reflect and plan.

General Reflection and Planning

Planning is not just a verbal activity. Teachers write their plans down so that they can remember their intentions and share them with others (colleagues, administrators, families). They may write down the goals and materials available in the different play areas of the classroom. They may note the songs to sing and books to read with children at large-group gatherings. They may discuss ways to enhance daily routines in the classroom so that every minute of the children's day is full of learning possibilities. Teachers may design their own planning frameworks or use published ones. As I shared in chapter 3, there

are three designs (for infants and toddlers, for preschoolers, and for kindergartners) in my book *Planning for Play, Observation, and Learning in Preschool and
Kindergarten* (2013). You can find the preschool design in appendix B. All three
of these frameworks are also available to download from www.redleafpress.org.

Many teachers write down what they will do with children in different areas
and activities but do not necessarily note the reflective part of their planning
conversations. In the frameworks in my book, a reflection page is included to
guide teachers in reviewing the previous week and planning for the necessary
changes for the next one. Here is the reflection page included in the planning
frameworks for all three of the age groups mentioned above.

Preschool Weekly Planning and Reflection Framework
OBSERVATIONS, MODIFICATIONS, AND REFLECTIONS

FOCUSED OBSERVATIONS:	MODIFICATIONS FOR INDIVIDUAL CHILDREN:
REFLECTIONS: What worked? What didn't? What did you learn about individual children and group interests?	**PLANS:** Based on your reflections, what will you change for next week?

Notice the critical questions asked in the reflection page above.

1 What worked?
2 What did not work?
3 What did you learn about individual children and group interests?

These questions can be applied to the whole group and to individual children.
After answering them, teachers move on to planning: "Based on your reflections, what will you change for next week?" If something worked well with

the group or with certain individuals, there is no need to change it! Weekly planning does not mean that teachers need to change every possible activity or experience for the next week. Young children love to repeat things they enjoy or do well. They bring to the experience something new in their confidence or in new skills or understandings. The things identified in reflection that did not work do need to be changed. Perhaps a quick and easy adjustment is all that is necessary. Look at the following reflection from a teaching team's conversation and the simple change they planned to overcome the problem.

As Mariah and Gail sat together to discuss how the previous week had gone and to plan for the next week, they remembered how lots of sand spilled out of the sensory table. They worried that it was a safety hazard and did not see children taking any steps to clean it up. They decided to add two small whisk brooms and dustpans, and two child-sized brooms to the area. They planned to introduce the tools to the children and encourage them to clean up as spills occurred. Their reflection a week later showed that the addition of these cleanup tools was successful—children loved sweeping up the sand and worked together to place it back in the sensory table.

At times, the unsuccessful activity or planned experience needs to be changed completely. Here is an example of a reflection from a teaching team's conversation and the changes they planned.

Jason and Teresa sat together planning for the next week. Much of their discussion focused on the lack of interest in the dramatic play area. For several weeks it had been set up as family living, with typical kitchen items and baby dolls for dressing and feeding. They had noticed that several children were talking about their pets at home and decided to ask the children if they would like to convert the dramatic play area into a veterinary clinic. They planned to invite children to suggest materials needed, to bring in stuffed animals from home, and to provide photos of their pets. They introduced the idea to the children first thing the following week with very enthusiastic responses. Veterinary clinic play continued in the classroom for several weeks along with a field trip to an actual clinic, a visit from a blind dog, and class books created about children's pets.

The reflective conversation among teaching colleagues can involve considering the needs of the whole group, as above, and it can focus on individual children's needs as well. Sometimes an activity or experience was not successful for one or two children. The planned changes for the next week may focus on ways to help those children, not to change the activity or experience. Here's an example of such a situation.

In their planning meeting, Shawna and Marie discussed a consistent problem that arose the previous week in their class library reading area. Many children chose to go to the area and look at books either alone or with a partner or two. However, each day, Brody and Kyle would run into the library, tripping over children seated there, and pull books out of the shelves, tossing them on the floor, laughing loudly, and running back out to another part of the room. The teachers intervened each time and redirected the boys, but the same thing happened each day. Shawna and Marie wondered if Brody and Kyle really wanted to join in the reading experience but didn't have the social skills or self-regulation to do so on their own. They planned to be proactive and preventative the next week and invite the boys to come to the library area with a teacher and read with her. They also considered the boys' interests and had seen their fascination with trucks and construction vehicles. They found books about those and planned to introduce those as special books just for Brody and Kyle. Their reflection the next week showed great success as long as a teacher was there with the boys. Other children also gathered and listened and looked at the books. Brody and Kyle were able to sit with other children and the teacher, looking at the pictures and sharing their expertise about the names of the many vehicles.

Reflection questions about what is working and what is not are an important part of weekly planning. They guide the discussion and help teachers consider group and individual successes and challenges and determine any changes that are necessary. But, periodically, a deep reflection about each individual child will lead a teacher to planning that will address the child's strengths, interests, and developmental needs.

Individualized Reflection and Planning

As we create our Developmental Studies that lead us to more individualized curriculum, we will use a format called the Developmental Study Teacher Reflection Form. Following is a copy of the blank form. You can find a full-sized copy of this in appendix B or download a PDF version from www.redleafpress.org.

Developmental Study Teacher Reflection Form

Child's Name:_____   Teacher:_____   Reflection Date(s:)_____

What can and does this child do? What specific skills does s/he have?

What would the next steps be for this child in his or her development?

What are his or her interests and how does s/he show them?

What will you plan to do with this child to build on his or her strengths and interests and to work on next steps?

What materials, activities, teacher support, peer support, and special resources will you use?

You can see that there are five questions for teachers to consider as they reflect about a child. For this reflection, they turn to the evidence they have collected in their ongoing research: the documented observations in the child's portfolio and any other documentation (such as Quick Check Recording Sheets, Small-Group Observation Forms, brief notes, photos, and work samples). They also enrich the reflection with their own memories. Once again, this kind of reflection is more informative when a teaching team engages in a focused discussion so that different perspectives enhance the reflection and help determine the next steps. Let's consider each of the reflective questions in this format and how teachers can use their documentation to help answer them.

The first question is "What can and does this child do? What specific skills does he or she have?" To answer this question, teachers turn to their documented observations on the portfolio forms and review the learning goals identified there. They then list these goals in the box provided on the reflection form. They can also turn to any other forms of documentation they have and add skills the child has demonstrated that they observed but may not have documented.

The second question is "What would the next steps be for this child in his or her development?" To answer, teachers must turn to their early learning standards or observational assessment tool and identify where the child is performing on the continuum of development related to specific skills. They then can see what comes next related to that skill. For example, Jeremy recognizes some letters in his name, so the next step for him would be to recognize more or all of the letters. Isabella plays alongside other children, sometimes playing independently, sometimes watching what the others are doing. The next step for her would be to begin to play *with* other children. By identifying these next steps, teachers can now begin the planning process and determine what they will do to assist the child in moving forward in that developmental area or particular skill.

The third question asks, "What are his or her interests, and how does he or she show them?" Teachers who have conducted Child Interest Surveys can review the child's responses and note them here. And they can look at the choice records they have completed. They can also consider if any other interests or favorites have become evident as they have observed the child over time. Perhaps the child went on a family trip to a museum and now shows great interest in dinosaurs or saw an animated movie and acts out favorite scenes almost word for word.

The fourth question leads teachers to use the information they recorded in answer to the first three questions: "What will you plan to do with this child to build on his or her strengths and interests and to work on next steps?" As teachers make plans for individual children, they look back at the child's developmental capabilities and interests to determine what to do to best meet the child's needs. Interests are included as a way to motivate children. Why not capitalize on what delights and interests the child in order to work on the next steps in his development? Why not delight in what the child delights in?

Let's consider the two children discussed above. Jeremy's teachers may plan to do activities with name cards, name puzzles, and name games. If Jeremy is the same child who also showed interest in dinosaurs, they may relate some letter identification activities to dinosaurs. If Isabella is the child who acts out favorite movie scenes, the teachers may plan to help her invite other children to join in and let her pretend to be the "movie director," assigning roles and gathering props to help stage the scene correctly.

The final question on the Developmental Study Teacher Reflection Form helps teachers identify practical considerations on how best to implement their plan: "What materials, activities, teacher support, peer support, and special resources will you use?" For Jeremy, teachers would need to make sure they have plenty of name cards created and plan for the various activities. They would also want to provide dinosaur books and help Jeremy identify the letters in the dinosaur names, maybe even making dinosaur name cards. There may be other children who show similar interests who could be invited to join in these activities. For Isabella, teachers would want to choose peers who will be willing to engage with her in dramatic play. The teachers would need to be ready to assist Isabella in playing with the other children, perhaps coaching her in ways to approach children and invite them to join in with her.

This in-depth reflection provides a way for teachers to pull together all of their documentation and internal knowledge about a child and use it to better teach the child.

> "I have used the Developmental Study Teacher Reflection Forms all along. I did the forms for all of my children and attached them to my IEPs. They were very helpful with my quarterly reports." —Cathy

> "I have decided to fill out the Developmental Study Teacher Reflection Forms earlier and use in our first conferences with families. Then I will continue to update them throughout the year. I can easily add pieces as we go (and maybe color code the additions)." —Danielle

Here are examples of two completed Developmental Study Teacher Reflection Forms. You can also review the Developmental Study Teacher Reflection Forms in the two Developmental Studies in appendix A to see how teachers reflected about and planned for individual children.

Developmental Study Teacher Reflection Form

Child's Name: **Emily**   Teacher: **Cathy**   Reflection Date(s:) **1/22, 1/30**

What can and does this child do? What specific skills does s/he have?
Listens to/watches stories that are read/signed; uses 1 word/sign to label things; can draw pictures from story and tell/sign what story character said. Is becoming aware of how words are spelled. Drew picture, said it was "Daddy" and then said "Daddy begins with *D*." Has begun to use more signs so she can be understood. Fingerspells first and last name.

What would the next steps be for this child in his or her development?
- Work on printing first name
- Sequence left to right
- Recognizing more beginning letters in spelling of words
- Continue to engage in stories and show understanding

What are his or her interests and how does s/he show them?
- Loves books – "reads" to her dolls and asks teachers to read/sign books.
- Has been interacting with new child in dramatic play in housekeeping area and during gross motor in gym

What will you plan to do with this child to build on his or her strengths and interests and to work on next steps?
- Work with speech pathologist for speech
- Encourage and model interacting with peers (especially new student)
- Require more language to get needs and wants met

What materials, activities, teacher support, peer support, and special resources will you use?
Books, pictures, markers, letter cards

Collaborate with speech pathologist

Developmental Study Teacher Reflection Form

Child's Name: **Ben**   Teacher: **Sara**   Reflection Date(s:) **2/10**

What can and does this child do? What specific skills does s/he have?
Verbally expresses himself; recognizes all upper and 13 lowercase letters; writes first and last name; writes and spells some words using phonetic spelling; counts up to 14 objects using 1-1; makes connections between home and school

What would the next steps be for this child in his or her development?
- Take risks/attempt to spell and write more without asking for "correct" spelling
- Recognize the names of friends and other common environmental print
- Solve basic problems involving quantities
- Focus on and complete a basic puzzle

What are his or her interests and how does s/he show them?
- Weather and geography – shared information he has learned
- Making books (drawing pictures)
- Dramatic play – especially store scenario

What will you plan to do with this child to build on his or her strengths and interests and to work on next steps?
- Use weather/geography topics to encourage bookmaking with words and pictures
- Make counting and math books
- Bring weather-and-geography related puzzles to class
- Create picture/name matching game
- Encourage other dramatic play scenarios and bring writing and math to both

What materials, activities, teacher support, peer support, and special resources will you use?
Ask preschool science teacher and early childhood librarian for weather-related materials and tools
Find weather-and-geography related puzzles
Help him "price" items in store – serve as cashier and do basic addition to add up quantities

The Frequency of Reflection

As I stated earlier in this chapter, teachers reflect all of the time. As they engage with children, they continually observe and evaluate the success of activities and experiences. And they make spontaneous decisions to change something right in the moment. But how often should teachers engage in the in-depth, individualized reflection as outlined in the Developmental Study Teacher Reflection Form?

At least once during a school year, teachers should consider answering these questions about the children with whom they work. As you can see, this reflection requires that a set of documented observations be completed, so the timing of this individualized reflection should occur after the completion of the child's fall portfolio. Midyear, such as the month of January, is a good time to set aside for this process. Rather than collecting more documentation during this month, teachers can focus on these kinds of reflective conversations. They can change "hats" and not be observers and documenters (for portfolio purposes) but rather, be in the reflective mode, contemplating what they have learned about each child and what they will plan next for each one.

Some teachers coordinate their reflection with a midyear family/teacher conference. They share with the family the completed fall portfolio forms as well as their conclusions on the Developmental Study Teacher Reflection Form. And they invite the family members' reflections about their child's capabilities and progress. They may even encourage the family to plan things they can do at home with their child to address next steps and to build on his interests. This is an example of the partnering that can take place between early educators and children's family members. They are all working together for the benefit of the child, sharing information, seeing documented observations, and planning next steps.

Conclusion

Teachers take on many roles as they work with young children. Reflection and planning based on that reflection are some of the most important things they can do to make sure all children are fully engaged in their learning. Periodically engaging in deep reflection about individual children will help teachers to know children better and to adapt curricular strategies for each one in ways that help the child be successful. In the next chapter, we will build on the reflective process and explore ways to address individualized goals in planning.

Planning for Individualized Goals

As teachers spend more time with children, their knowledge of each child deepens. They can often take one look at a child as she walks into the classroom in the morning and recognize that something is off.

- Perhaps she looks sleepy because she stayed up later than usual.
- Perhaps car problems on the way to school were upsetting for both the child and her family members.
- Perhaps his throat is sore and he is not feeling up to par.
- Perhaps he sees that another child has a favorite toy that he hoped to play with as he arrived at school.

While they engage with children throughout each day, teachers continue to build their understanding of children's strengths, personality traits, interests, talents, and areas of challenge.

Teachers can use their knowledge about individual children to plan activities and experiences that address goals specific to each child's needs. But they may feel overwhelmed if they try to address every goal they identified on the reflection forms for each child. To avoid such feelings, teachers can use two strategies to help them plan curriculum that relates to goals for individual children:

1. They can prioritize and consider which goals are most important for each child.
2. They can identify other children who will benefit from activities and experiences that address those goals.

Individualization does not necessarily mean planning a different goal for each child in a group of twenty children! There are more practical and realistic ways to individualize planning. In this chapter, I will introduce you to three formats for individualized goal planning: the Individualized Goal Planning Sheet, Modifications for Individual Children, and the Individual Adjustments Form.

The Individualized Goal Planning Sheet

The first format is called the Individualized Goal Planning Sheet. Here is a copy of the blank form. You can find a full-sized copy of this sheet in appendix B or download a PDF version from www.redleafpress.org.

Individualized Goal Planning Sheet

Child's Name:_____   Date:_____   Teacher:_____

Developmental Learning Goals for This Child:	Other Children Who Would Benefit from These Goals:
1.	1.
2.	2.

Plans for Experiences to Work toward These Goals with This Child:
(What play area[s], materials, peer groupings, and teacher support strategies will you plan?)

Results of Implementation of Plan:

For this child:

For the other children:

Each time a teacher uses this format, he chooses two developmental learning goals informed by the completed Developmental Study Teacher Reflection Form. In that reflection, he probably identified more than two goals taken from his state early learning standards or the assessment tool that his program uses. However, in order to focus planning, he chooses two of them that he considers most important for the child at this time.

> "The Individualized Goal Planning Sheet has helped the teacher whom I am coaching to think more out of the box. It's really helping him to think about how to use the standards." —Teresa

"By writing individualized plans related to the Ohio standards, I got to know the standards so much better. It was a nice way to help us learn the new standards and relate them to our children." —Linda

In addition, this format asks the teacher to think beyond this one child and identify other children who might benefit from activities that address the same two goals. Teachers can then expand their planning to include other members of the group and will not need to complete an Individualized Goal Planning Sheet for every child. They may complete two or three at a time for different small groups of children.

"We're really thinking about other children who would benefit from these goals. For example, I thought of four other children who absolutely needed help with letter identification." —Jordan

"This kind of goal planning helps me think more and have a complete picture to help individual students in their development and progress." —Mark

"I really liked the Individualized Goal Planning Sheet. I realized that I could set a goal that would last for a quarter. It made it much better to plan that way. And it helped me identify the other students who would benefit as well." —Kelly

Here are two examples of completed Individualized Goal Planning Sheets. They do not yet include the results of the implementation of the plans. You can also review the Individualized Goal Planning Sheets in the two Developmental Studies in appendix A to see how teachers made use of this format.

Individualized Goal Planning Sheet

Child's Name: __Mariah__   Date: __2/3__   Teacher: __Brett__

Developmental Learning Goals for This Child:

1. Write first name.
2. Use appropriate words to initiate play with peers (with teacher support).

Other Children Who Would Benefit from These Goals:

Andrea and Bridget (build on Mariah's new connections with them)

Plans for Experiences to Work toward These Goals with This Child:
(What play area[s], materials, peer groupings, and teacher support strategies will you plan?)

1. Alphabet stamps, dot-dot markers, rainbow writing
2. Look at books with friends.
3. Role play with friends in dramatic play area.
4. Read social stories and play games where she supplies words for social scenarios.

Results of Implementation of Plan:

For this child:

For the other children:

Individualized Goal Planning Sheet

Child's Name: __Darla__   Date: __1/28__   Teacher: __Cathy__

Developmental Learning Goals for This Child:

1. Use word/sign to communicate needs and wants.
2. Move from parallel to more interactive play with peers.

Other Children Who Would Benefit from These Goals:

1. Elliot, Jonah, Marie
2. Missy, James, Celeste

Plans for Experiences to Work toward These Goals with This Child:
(What play area[s], materials, peer groupings, and teacher support strategies will you plan?)

1. Give choice of two objects and give sign for each, then have children sign which one they want.
2. Give more wait time during breakfast, lunch, and snack so children will sign asking for help, for more, or for what they want.
3. Model ways to engage with peers in dramatic play area.
4. Encourage cooperation in drawing a group mural, acting out a favorite story, and playing group games like Duck, Duck, Goose.

Results of Implementation of Plan:

For this child:

For the other children:

Along with individualized goal planning, teachers continue to use a planning framework for the whole group, as I showed in chapter 3. They address the needs of *all* of the children through both group and individualized planning. They set goals for play areas for the whole group. They identify needed materials for small-group experiences and plans for large-group gatherings. In addition, they pay attention to individualized goals and planning strategies to help the children for whom those goals are appropriate.

The goals teachers identify for the whole group are generally broader than the ones for an individual child. For example, for the dramatic play area, the goal for the whole group might be "engages in role play." While for the individual child (and the small group who will also benefit), the goal might be "converses with others, listening and responding." To successfully engage in role play, children *do* need to converse—but for this particular child (and the identified others), that is the next step for her in her language development. Role play will be the way to get at that more specific goal.

When to Complete the Individualized Goal Planning Sheets

Individualized goal planning is a direct result of in-depth teacher reflection. Therefore, it comes after completion of the Developmental Study Teacher Reflection Form. If teachers engage in a deep reflection about each child in January, then they will complete the Individualized Goal Planning Sheets at the end of that month or in early February. The individualized plans set forth will continue over several weeks, during which teachers will have plenty of opportunities to observe children engaged in the activities and experiences they planned related to the goals. Here are the results of the above plans for Mariah and Darla.

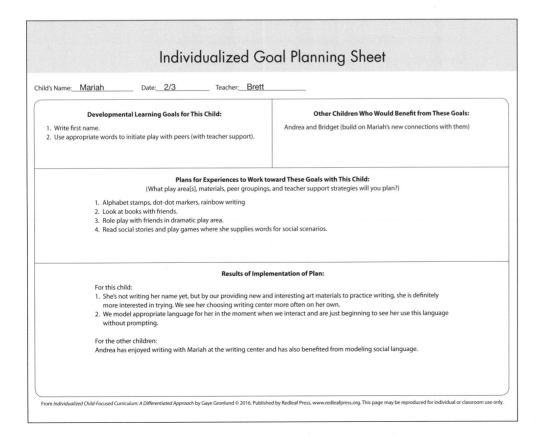

Individualized Goal Planning Sheet

Child's Name: Mariah   Date: 2/3   Teacher: Brett

Developmental Learning Goals for This Child:	Other Children Who Would Benefit from These Goals:
1. Write first name. 2. Use appropriate words to initiate play with peers (with teacher support).	Andrea and Bridget (build on Mariah's new connections with them)

Plans for Experiences to Work toward These Goals with This Child:
(What play area[s], materials, peer groupings, and teacher support strategies will you plan?)

1. Alphabet stamps, dot-dot markers, rainbow writing
2. Look at books with friends.
3. Role play with friends in dramatic play area.
4. Read social stories and play games where she supplies words for social scenarios.

Results of Implementation of Plan:

For this child:
1. She's not writing her name yet, but by our providing new and interesting art materials to practice writing, she is definitely more interested in trying. We see her choosing writing center more often on her own.
2. We model appropriate language for her in the moment when we interact and are just beginning to see her use this language without prompting.

For the other children:
Andrea has enjoyed writing with Mariah at the writing center and has also benefited from modeling social language.

Individualized Goal Planning Sheet

Child's Name:__Darla_____   Date:__1/28_____   Teacher:__Cathy_____

Developmental Learning Goals for This Child:

1. Use word/sign to communicate needs and wants.
2. Move from parallel to more interactive play with peers.

Other Children Who Would Benefit from These Goals:

1. Elliot, Jonah, Marie
2. Missy, James, Celeste

Plans for Experiences to Work toward These Goals with This Child:
(What play area[s], materials, peer groupings, and teacher support strategies will you plan?)

1. Give choice of two objects and give sign for each, then have children sign which one they want.
2. Give more wait time during breakfast, lunch, and snack so children will sign asking for help, for more, or for what they want.
3. Model ways to engage with peers in dramatic play area.
4. Encourage cooperation in drawing a group mural, acting out a favorite story, and playing group games like Duck, Duck, Goose.

Results of Implementation of Plan:

For this child:
1. She has independently begun to ask for more and say please by signing.
2. She joins in with us as we play with children but does not initiate cooperation or interaction unless guided to do so.

For the other children:
1. Elliot and Marie are signing more than ever; Marie is doing some when prompted.
2. Missy and Celeste are engaging in some cooperative play. James tends to observe nearby.

To use the Individualized Goal Planning Sheet to its fullest, teachers need to think about planning for play areas, materials, peer groupings, and teacher support strategies with children's individual needs in mind. Let's look at each of these categories in more depth.

Considerations for Planning Play Areas

Teachers consider several different environmental factors when planning to work on developmental goals with children in play areas of the classroom:

- the physical arrangement of the play area
- the amount of space available and how many children it will comfortably accommodate
- the organized display and availability of materials

Planning for the environment is an important part of providing a sense of structure for children so that their play experiences will be productive ones with many learning possibilities. Teachers are thoughtful and intentional as they organize shelves and tables to create clearly defined play areas. And they are flexible and ready to change the environment as they observe where children are successful in play and where problems arise.

> The room arrangement and presentation of materials communicate important messages to the children. Those messages deeply affect behavior. If the classroom is messy and disorganized, children will probably not take good care of the materials...if materials are carefully organized and presented in a clear, appealing fashion, children may treat them with more care and put them away more easily at cleanup time. If shelving and tables are used to create specific learning areas throughout the room and placed in a way that breaks up running paths and creates intimate spaces for using certain materials, children will settle down and become engaged with activities for longer periods of time and with more productive ends. (Gronlund 2013, 26)

While the environment is planned with the whole group in mind, there are ways to organize play areas to meet individual children's needs. Here are some examples:

Individual Need: Some children are sensitive to the invasion of their personal space. Even in a play area with plenty of square footage, some children worry about protecting what they are building or creating. They are easily bothered by the presence of others nearby.

Planning Strategy: Teachers can recognize these children's needs by defining a work space for them. At a table, this might be a placemat or cafeteria-style tray that sits in front of the child to define a space for his materials. On the floor, the teacher can provide string or yarn and help the child measure out a reasonable space within which he can work. Or she can put down a vinyl tablecloth or piece of fabric to set up a protected and defined area for play.

Individual Need: Some children have favorite play areas and do not choose others. Since teachers know that each area in the environment provides different kinds of opportunities for engagement and learning, they may worry that these children seem "stuck" and are not benefiting from the full experience available to them.

Planning Strategy: At St. Saviour's Church Nursery School in Old Greenwich, Connecticut, teachers implemented a "Golden Ticket" approach that was extremely successful in encouraging children to try unfamiliar play areas. At least once weekly, teachers created Golden Tickets that identified a play area and the names of several children who would begin playing there together. Children were asked to stay for twenty minutes (chimes were rung at that time) and then could choose to move to other play choices if they wanted. Teachers "chose centers that would mix the familiar places where the children played with the unfamiliar. They also mixed the peers with whom children could interact so children could share their knowledge with a wider group and have opportunities to find interests they shared" (Gronlund and Stewart 2013, 115). Teachers reported success as children explored unfamiliar areas and began to choose them for play on days when there were no Golden Tickets.

Individual Need: Each child has unique characteristics that can be addressed in the environment.

Planning Strategy: In the journal *Teaching Young Children*, Laura J. Colker offers a regular set of suggestions for individualizing learning centers. In one article, she suggests the following strategies in order to support all children's needs:

- Create a place for quiet work.
- Adapt materials and tools (so all children can work independently).
- Teach children how to use equipment.
- Consider home languages (post written labels, children's dictations, and word walls in children's home languages).
- Let children know their work is important and appreciated by designating a space for unfinished work (with a Please Save or Under Construction sign) and a display space for finished work to be admired (as in creating a class museum). (Colker 2015)

Teachers can check out other issues of this journal for additional ideas for individualizing play areas.

Considerations for Planning Materials

When teachers plan for the basic sets of materials to provide in the different play areas for the whole group, they think about materials that are inviting and full of many possibilities. They make sure there are enough items for several children to simultaneously engage in productive play in the area. They consider how to organize those materials in baskets and bins and how to display them on the shelves so children can easily access them. They may label the shelves and baskets with photos of the materials (and words, if appropriate) for easy cleanup. "Order is communicated clearly to children by this arrangement. As children are using materials and putting them away by themselves, they develop independence and a sense of responsibility" (Gronlund 2013, 105).

Teachers usually do not change the basic sets of materials available in the play areas very often—only when necessary based on their observations of the children's engagement. The following circumstances warrant a change in materials:

- The children are ignoring a particular area.
- The children are bored with what is available (they may say they are bored; they may appear bored in their interactions; or they may change the area themselves, bringing new materials or doing different things with those materials).
- The children's behavior is not productive or positive in an area.
- The materials could be changed to support an interest of the children, a developmental need, or a topic of study or project that has emerged in the classroom. (Gronlund 2013, 111)

When planning for individualized learning goals, teachers may use the existing materials in a play area, or they may provide different ones related to the goals involved. Here are two examples that illustrate different individualized strategies about materials related to the learning goal of "uses emergent writing skills."

In our kindergarten classroom, I introduced the children to the idea of stapling papers together to make books. This has become very popular and resulted in many more students writing. Today Evan went to the writing center and took loose sheets of paper, stacked them, folded them, and asked me for the stapler. "I'm making a book," he announced. On the first page, he began writing and drawing, then stopped and called to me, "How do you spell 'world record book'?" I was working with a couple of other students and said I'd help him in a few minutes. When I was ready to help him, he had gone back to the table and was engaged in writing and drawing on several pages. He worked for fifteen minutes and then brought his book and read it to me: "World Record Book; World's Largest Piece of Paper; World's Largest Muffin; World's Biggest Apple; World's Biggest Skateboard."

In our preschool room of three-year-olds, we have some very intense block builders, but they do not tend to choose the writing areas we have in the classroom. So I decided to bring writing to them! At group meeting, I introduced them to the work of architects and showed them some actual blueprints of building plans. Then I offered to provide blue paper (and other colors as well) and writing tools in the block area so that the builders there could make their own plans before they built a structure or after it was already built. On the first few days, I stayed in the block area to model ways to design the blueprints and include writing about the structures. Although my three-year-olds mostly made marks, letter-like shapes, and sometimes their names, they certainly engaged in much more use of writing tools with the purpose of making their own blueprints. Now we have their plans hanging all around the block area.

Teachers of young children need to think in terms of each child's capabilities and plan their materials accordingly. Here are several examples of individualizing with materials.

Individual Need: The child has a physical disability and is unable to stand on her own.

Planning Strategy: Provide a stander so that she can join other children at the sensory table or other table activities.

Individual Need: The child has issues with his fine-motor skills.

Planning Strategy: Provide large beads for stringing; puzzle pieces with handles; and markers that flow easily in the writing and art areas.

Individual Need: The child is a dual-language learner.

Planning Strategy: Provide books, posters, and labels in the child's home language as well as English; use the child's home language in conversation with the child as much as possible.

Individual Need: The child is deeply interested in trains (or whatever).

Planning Strategy: Use trains and train-related materials to address learning goals in all domains for this child: offer opportunities to read, write, and talk about trains, to count the number of train cars, to measure the length of train tracks, to identify shapes related to trains, to explore scientific principles of friction and speed and momentum with trains, to play with others in role-playing train trips.

One other point needs to be made when considering individual adaptations to play areas and the materials available: Choose areas and materials that match the developmental goals identified. Do not try to meet the goals in areas where it is not easily done. In other words, use common sense and do not make extra work for yourself.

> Again, remember, it is not necessary to coordinate every activity in the classroom with a topic! Don't rack your brain trying to come up with materials in every area that relate [to a child's or group of children's interests]. Instead, plan for activities that are meaningful and make sense. The rest of the classroom environment will stand as the rich and inviting place that it is. (Gronlund 2013, 153)

Considerations for Planning Peer Groupings

Teachers often individualize by partnering children in different ways. Children gravitate to friends with similar interests and may do so with children with similar capabilities and life experiences. However, there may be times that teachers want to address developmental goals by creating new groupings of children. These strategies can be a way to provide support and comfort for a child, or to offer a provocation that may encourage the child to engage with peers with whom he is not as familiar. This is a form of teacher intentionality.

> Effective teachers attend to individual and group dynamics. From observing children's comfort levels and preferences with various groupings, they can plan strategies to ensure that each child feels secure and supported in trying out new or uncomfortable situations. (Epstein 2007, 14)

Teachers can identify partners for children based on their developmental strengths, home languages, interests, or social skills. Remember our story about the teachers who used the Golden Ticket strategy? They not only encouraged children to explore different play areas, but they intentionally chose play partners for the children.

Of the three or four children assigned to a center, the teachers made sure one was a frequent visitor to that area and the others infrequent. Their intention was for the child who was familiar with the materials to take on the role of leader—a new role for some children. . . . The teachers' thoughtful groupings of children opened the door to new partnerships as the children made new connections with classmates while using unfamiliar materials. . . . And children who were reticent with peers in teacher-led group times now freely shared their expertise with classmates while comfortably engaged with familiar materials. This allowed their classmates to see them in a new light. (Gronlund and Stewart 2013, 115–17)

By partnering children in different groupings, teachers encourage peer coaching. Perhaps a child is more experienced and expressive in dramatic play than others. Encouraging this child to join with play partners who are less verbal or who may be dual-language learners can provide a situation where children will follow another child's lead. Children who have strong cognitive skills may be able to teach children without the same depth of understanding, for example, by providing the counting words as partners attempt to count higher and higher quantities of objects.

Here are some examples of partnering strategies used by teachers to address individualized developmental goals.

> To address our goal for Devin regarding connecting to individual children, we are planning to offer small-group play experiences around topics of interest to a like-minded group of children (Peter, Aaron, and Garrison). We'll start with construction vehicles because they've all shown great interest in the bulldozers clearing the lot across the street from our school.

> In our classroom full of both mono- and dual-language learners, we often see the children playing only with the children who speak their home language. We decided to try to stimulate more cross groupings by suggesting that a mixed group pretend to give a birthday party for one of our Spanish-speaking teachers. Since birthday parties are always popular, the children readily agreed, and soon the birthday song was being sung in both English and Spanish. Children with differing home languages were helping each other "decorate" a playdough cake, drape scarves and streamers around the classroom for "decorations," and wrap empty boxes as "presents."

Considerations for Planning Teacher Support Strategies

As mentioned in chapter 8, teachers take on many roles in the classroom. And no matter what they are focusing on at any one time, they are always supporting the children. Some support strategies lend themselves to individualized developmental goals. Let's consider the following three teacher strategies:

1 Celebrating children's accomplishments
2 Scaffolding children's learning
3 Providing provocations or challenges

Young children love recognition from the important people in their lives, and teachers are certainly important to them! Therefore, any time their teacher recognizes and celebrates what they have done, children feel encouraged to continue. When a teacher sets a developmental goal for a child, she may be choosing something that is just beyond the child's present capability, so she wants to make sure she recognizes what the child *can* do before she works with her toward the next step in her development. In this way, the teacher builds the child's confidence and readiness to tackle something more challenging.

Here are some ways teachers can celebrate children's accomplishments:

- Tell the child what they have noticed that he *can* do or is learning to do.
- Photograph or videotape what the child is doing.
- Ask the child to demonstrate for others or help them do the same thing.
- Announce to the class what they have noticed (some teachers even use a handmade toilet paper roll microphone and act as a news reporter!).
- Have a special place to display creations, photos, and work samples.
- Share the child's accomplishments with her family members (in conversation at drop-off or pickup time, in a phone call or e-mail, or in portfolio documentation).

A confident child is ready to tackle new challenges with her teacher's assistance. This is where scaffolding comes in. Teachers provide support and assistance to children when needed and then work toward removing that support when the children are able to do something on their own.

> As a child begins a new challenge, he may need some support from the teacher to enable him to manage it. A skilled teacher doesn't overdo the help. The aim is to provide the least amount of support that the child needs to do something he cannot quite do on his own. . . . As the child begins to acquire the new skill or understanding, the teacher gradually reduces her support. (Copple and Bredekamp 2009, 39)

When teachers set developmental goals for children in specific domains and related to specific skills, they are identifying where to go next with them. But they must pay careful attention to the children's reaction as they introduce these next steps. They need to find the right amount of challenge and offer the right amount of support to each child. This can be tricky!

> The teacher needs "to identify the amount of challenge that is just right for each child so that she continues to try the new skill or understand the new concept. If the challenge is too hard, the child may give up, feel overwhelmed, get frustrated, or withdraw. If the challenge is too easy, the child may become uninterested, become bored, misbehave, or give up and withdraw." (Gronlund 2013, 141)

If the teacher determines that the challenge is too hard, he can provide assistance, model, demonstrate, or change the activity altogether. If he finds that it is too easy for the child, he can consider ways to make it more complex. Throughout his planning for individualized developmental goals, he is continually thinking how he will support the child, provide scaffolding when needed, and work toward independent accomplishment of the goals identified.

Provocations can be another way to work with children toward individualized goals. Teachers are not trying to provoke children to anger or frustration, but rather are attempting to open up possibilities—to provoke their thinking and bring about greater engagement (Kantor and Whaley 1998). A teacher can even ask a child or small group of children, "Would you like a challenge?" and create a sense of excitement as she says something like "I wonder what you could build if you used all of the blocks?"

Provocations can include any of the following:

- introducing new materials
- suggesting new ways to use and/or combine materials
- encouraging children to plan for ways to use materials and to write or draw about those plans—then checking in when finished and evaluating how the plan turned out
- asking children to figure out ways to show others what they are doing (through a demonstration, a photo display or video, a drawing, or a documentation panel) and helping them to do so

Here are some examples of ways teachers provided provocations or challenges that addressed individualized development goals.

"I have begun 'challenges' for the three-year-olds in my class by providing them pictures in the block area to help stimulate building. The attached pictures are a week after the 'city challenge' was established. The two quietest girls in the class took on the challenge. Before we knew it, they had an amazing structure built. They even used the overhead projector to illuminate it and cast an amazing shadow of their city on the wall." —Pete

"In the past we placed the shelf with bins full of a variety of small manipulatives in a far corner of the room. However, recently we moved it right next to the block area and told the children, 'We wonder if you might find ways to use some of the items in the bins in your block structures. We're very curious to see what you do!' These photos show some of the wonderful results." —Laura

Two Formats for Weekly Modifications for Individual Children

The considerations for individualization that we looked at above were related to reflection and planning that might take place over several weeks. Teachers can also plan weekly for individual modifications. You may recall the reflection page from the Lesson Planning Framework shared in chapter 8. In our discussion, we focused on the questions posed to reflect on changes needed in planning. But another way to individualize planning is included on that page. Here is a blank copy of the reflection page. Let's look at ways to use this format with individualization in mind.

Preschool Weekly Planning and Reflection Framework
OBSERVATIONS, MODIFICATIONS, AND REFLECTIONS

FOCUSED OBSERVATIONS:	MODIFICATIONS FOR INDIVIDUAL CHILDREN:
REFLECTIONS: What worked? What didn't? What did you learn about individual children and group interests?	PLANS: Based on your reflections, what will you change for next week?

You can see that the box at the top right of the page is titled Modifications for Individual Children. This is another place where teachers can record their plans to help individual children reach developmental goals. In using this, teachers may not find it necessary to complete the Individualized Goal Planning Sheet. Instead, as they plan for each week, they will identify goals for next steps for individual children and specify the teaching strategies they will use to help children meet those goals. Here are two examples of completed plans for Modifications for Individual Children.

MODIFICATIONS FOR INDIVIDUAL CHILDREN:

Put out alphabet matching game (lower to upper case) as a challenge for all children but especially for Rebecca, Jason and Heather.

Give Jarrett a special assignment to measure the classroom, doorways, tables, etc. with Unifix cubes.

Provide emotional support for Stephanie for her fear of loud noises.

Watch for best seating at group times for Grecia and Ricardo—perhaps they should be separate from each other?

MODIFICATIONS FOR INDIVIDUAL CHILDREN:

Encourage Hillary, Mason, and Edward to invite more children into the camping dramatic play.

Offer some quiet table activities for Aiden during group time.

Both Josephine and Marie will allow extra time for Austin and David to respond and will set up opportunities for them to point or touch and speak whenever possible.

Another format to consider is the Individual Adjustments Form, which provides space for teachers to record individualized plans for many children. This form was originally designed by a special educator who used it to remind herself of children's IEP goals. Here is a copy of the blank form. You can find a full-sized copy of this format in appendix B, or you can download a PDF version from www.redleafpress.org.

Individual Adjustments

For week of: _____   Teacher: _____

Child's Name	Planned Adjustment	Child's Name	Planned Adjustment

You can see that there are spaces for sixteen children's names and the adjustments or curricular strategies for which a teacher would plan. Here is an example of a completed form. You can see that the space provided requires more brevity in the teacher's written plans.

Individual Adjustments

For week of: March 15   Teacher: Pam

Child's Name	Planned Adjustment	Child's Name	Planned Adjustment
Aiden	Due to his personal space issues, allow him to be special helper setting up snack during group time.	Naomi	Help her express feelings appropriately—pound a pillow? Use a puppet? Draw?
Brianna	Provide more early readers in library—she's ready!	Stephanie	Support her emerging leadership skills, especially outdoors.
Christian	Pair with Timothy and Evan at math area—encourage simple addition and subtraction.	Timothy	Math games with Christian and Evan.
Evan	Math games with Timothy and Christian.		
Gabriella	Provide more writing materials (create books or journals?)		
Henry	Be ready to support his participation at group time.		
Layla	Pair with Gabriella at writing center—see if that encourages more writing on her part.		
Michael	Provide more wait time for his responses (per recommendations of speech pathologist).		

A completed form like this might be attached to the group lesson plans and cover many weeks. The results of the adjustments (or of the modifications made on the reflection page) would be documented on the spring portfolio forms and in other documentation formats. Both of these methods of individualized goal planning lack the possibility of relating the plan to other children who might benefit. But they can easily be incorporated into weekly planning for the whole group. Teachers can decide what works best for them in addressing individual children's goals in curricular planning.

Conclusion

In individualized goal planning, teachers make adjustments to meet individual children's needs in the play area environments, materials, peer groupings, and teacher support strategies. In the next chapter, we will consider how to summarize children's learning for their families and plan effective family/teacher conferencing.

10 Preparing for Family/ Teacher Conferencing

Over time, teachers get to know all of the children in their early childhood program. They document what they learn about each child's interests and record observations that show the child's progress toward developmental goals. They communicate with the children's families in several ways: through face-to-face conversations, e-mails, newsletters, and announcements, or in telephone calls and texts. From time to time, they meet with families to review the documentation in the child's Developmental Study and share conclusions about the child's development and progress.

Shifting from Documentation to Evaluation

Before scheduling a time for a formal family/teacher conference, teachers need to shift gears from documenting evidence (as in the factual written descriptions of their observations) to evaluating that evidence. Remember, when documenting, the focus is on factual, descriptive, and objective language. When teachers evaluate their documentation, they use their judgment and determine where the child is strong and in what areas he needs more work. While they may have been doing this all along as they planned curricular activities for the children, when preparing to conference with families, they summarize what they have learned about the child. They can celebrate all of the child's accomplishments and use words like "He does a good job at. . . ." or "She really knows how to. . . ." They can also consider where problems arise for the child and what skills are not as well established. The evaluation process is a time to draw conclusions about how the child is growing, developing, and learning.

To move from documentation to evaluation, teachers need to take the following steps:

1 Stop collecting documentation (evaluating requires a different way of thinking—continuing to gather information may not allow a teacher to shift his viewpoint).

2 Review the documentation for each child domain by domain (portfolios, photographs, work samples, quick check, and other formats).

3 Add any undocumented information from memory about the child's performance in each domain.

4 Relate all of the information about the child to early learning standards or to indicators on assessment tools that are appropriate for the age of the child.

5 Determine where each child has shown growth and progress, what standards or indicators she has accomplished, and where she needs continued support and assistance.

6 Write summary reports for each child.

7 Schedule and conduct family/teacher conferences to share the portfolios and summaries.

These steps require a concentrated effort. Teachers need to devote time to deep reflection and review, allow for discussions with colleagues, and write the evaluation results. The written evaluation is shared with each child's family, and a copy is maintained in the child's records. It may also be shared with the following year's teacher (whether the child is transitioning within the program or moving on to a different setting, such as kindergarten).

"Every time I write narratives I discover a thousand things about my children. When you're sitting down at a table reviewing your anecdotal notes, photos, and data from the last six months that you've spent with the child, you reflect and see a whole child. You look back at what they were first doing and see the progress. This is the single, most helpful process." —Jordan

Two Summary Formats

During the evaluation stage and to complete the Developmental Study process, teachers can use two formats. The first format is the Developmental Study Teacher and Family Reflection Form. Here is a copy of the blank form. You can find a copy of this format in appendix B or download a PDF version from www. redleafpress.org.

Developmental Study Teacher and Family Reflection Form

Child's Name:_____   Age:_____   Date:_____   Teacher:_____

General Summary of the Child's Interests and Delights, Accomplishments, and Progress

Teacher:

Family Members:

This form provides an opportunity for teachers and family members to think about the whole child and what he has accomplished in his time at the early childhood program. This format allows the teacher to pull together all of the information and highlight some of the things she has learned about the child, has enjoyed in her work with him, and seen him accomplish. She can look across time and compare what the child is doing now to what he did earlier in the year. One way to consider writing this summary is to answer these questions:

- What in general do I want the family to know about the child and his experience at our program?
- How can I summarize what we have learned about him as a competent and capable little person?
- What can I celebrate about him?

Here are some examples of reflective summaries.

> Ethan has grown so much in the area of self-confidence in our kindergarten classroom. He's willing to say, "I can do that!" and doesn't need as much teacher support. He's become a reader and is much more interested in reading books on his own, figuring them out for himself. And, he's a writer. At the beginning of the year, he didn't see himself that way, but now he views himself as an author. Socially, he's grown a lot. He's learned to communicate with peers and express his feelings through words. This has really had a positive effect on his behavior. I have been delighted to see Ethan mature and learn so much!

> Solana seems to love school and arrives daily with a big smile on her face. She makes the days sunnier and happier in the classroom for everyone! Dramatic play is a favorite. In the fall, she played more independently and with no real plot to her play stories. Now there are story lines. She's cooperating with other children and using more materials to enhance the role play. One of the biggest changes I've seen for her socially is her ability to negotiate and solve problems with her peers. Cognitively, she's writing letters and her knowledge about print has grown substantially. And her math skills have grown. She has one-to-one correspondence when she counts and understands numbers. That's also an area of real growth.

The Developmental Study Teacher and Family Reflection Form also has space for the child's family members to contribute their own summary reflection about their child. This section can be filled out in conversation with the family at the family/teacher conference. Once the teacher has shared her written summary reflection, she can invite the family to add what they have observed in their child's growth over the last few months. The teacher can serve as the recorder, or she can invite the family to write on the form themselves. Some teachers send an inquiry home before the family/teacher conference asking families to write up or to come prepared to discuss what they see as the child's interests and delights, accomplishments, and progress. Teachers report that families greatly appreciate being asked to share information and thoughts about their child. Here are two examples of family responses.

We have seen Mingyu grow and learn so much in preschool this year. Her English is so much better! She speaks English at home sometimes, even to her grandmother who only speaks Mandarin. She loves the friends she plays with—Sonia, Clare, and Evan. Sonia has come to visit us, and Mingyu has played at her house too. We're happy that she can write her name and knows some of the letters. She likes us to read the same books as you read at school, and then she tells us what will happen next. Thank you.

I was concerned earlier in the year that Anton wasn't communicating verbally very much. He was pretty quiet at home, and I know you had mentioned he was at school as well, but that sure has changed. He talks much more to all of us in the family and uses longer sentences and explanations. We've seen that he's really interested in music and can keep a beat with the drum set that we have at home, even some pretty complicated rhythms. And he loves going to school. He wants to go on the weekends and keeps asking us when he can go again.

You can review the Developmental Study Teacher and Family Reflection Forms in the two Developmental Studies in appendix A to see how teachers made use of this format.

The second format to use in the evaluation process is the Family/Teacher Summary Report. This format is oriented to provide assessment information about the child's progress and accomplishments in each of the domains addressed in the early childhood program. A copy of the blank form is on the next page. You can find a copy of this format in appendix B or download a PDF version from www.redleafpress.org.

You can see that the report is divided into sections for the domains the teacher will be addressing. Within each domain, he writes information about the child's growth and accomplishments and what the teachers will continue to work on with the child. A teacher turns to the child's portfolio and any other documentation he has collected, as well as his memory, to complete each of the sections on this report. He reviews the learning goals identified on the portfolio forms and lists them in the appropriate domains. If he has evidence to support that the child is indeed accomplishing the goal, he writes it under growth and accomplishments. If his documentation shows significant progress, he notes that as well. And he writes, "See portfolio item" if there are items that support his conclusions.

Family-Teacher Summary Report

Child's Name: _____ Date: _____

Teacher: _____ Program: _____

DOMAIN:

Growth and accomplishments	
We will continue to work on	

DOMAIN:

Growth and accomplishments	
We will continue to work on	

DOMAIN:

Growth and accomplishments	
We will continue to work on	

(continued on next page)

If the teacher reviews the observational descriptions and other documentation pieces and concludes that a child is still working to accomplish a particular learning goal (standard or indicator), then he writes that one in the "We will continue to work on . . ." section for the domain. Or, for a learning goal that the child has accomplished, the teacher can turn to his early learning standards or assessment tool to determine what the next level of expectation is and note that in this section.

Please notice that the language in the report is not "The *child* needs to work on . . ." but rather emphasizes that the *teachers* will continue to work on the skills or concepts *with* the child. The responsibility lies with the adults, not with the child. Therefore, in conversation with families at the conference time it's easy to add a suggestion such as "At home, you could help by. . . ." Teachers can give them ideas for home activities related to the goals they are working on and invite families to suggest some ideas of their own. In this way, teachers and families are working in partnership to plan goals for the child.

Here are two examples of the first page of completed Family/Teacher Summary Reports. In addition, you can review the Family/Teacher Summary Reports in the two Developmental Studies in appendix A to see how teachers made use of this format.

Family-Teacher Summary Report

Child's Name: Kendall　　　　　　　　　　　Date: 4-25

Teacher: Mark　　　　　　　　　Program: Pre-K

DOMAIN: Approaches to Learning

Growth and accomplishments	Kendall has learned to set goals for herself and remain on task as she works toward achieving them.
We will continue to work on	maintaining her sense of curiosity about learning new things about herself and her environment and provide positive feedback/encouragement when she's frustrated about a task she has set for herself!

DOMAIN: Mathematics

Growth and accomplishments	Kendall has very competent counting skills, shape recognition, and one-to-one correspondence. She can replicate patterns, understands spatial relationships, and measure length and width.
We will continue to work on	encouraging math exploration by providing frequent opportunities to count items and start playing with addition and subtraction problems with real items.

DOMAIN: Social Studies

Growth and accomplishments	By exploring a globe and becoming familiar with multicultural pictures and items, Kendall has developed an understanding of cultural similarities and differences.
We will continue to work on	encouraging Kendall to make personal maps (home, neighborhood, playground) and providing access to books (fiction and non-fiction) depicting world cultures.

(continued on next page)

Family-Teacher Summary Report

Child's Name: __Samile__   Date: __5-10__

Teacher: __Brett__   Program: __Preschool__

DOMAIN: Language and Literacy

Growth and accomplishments	Samile is starting to write his first name in full with recognizable letters most of the time. He recognizes his own name and that of many of his peers. His spoken vocabulary is extensive and he engages in full conversations with give-and-take with others. He loves to look at books and does so regularly.
We will continue to work on	encouraging his writing, supporting his oral language, and building on his interest in books.

DOMAIN: Mathematics

Growth and accomplishments	Samile has good number sense and shows more confidence in counting with one-to-one (at this point up to 5). He notices similarities and differences with shapes as he builds in the block area but does not name shapes yet. He joins in measurement comparisons when done, with teacher prompting.
We will continue to work on	encouraging continued math exploration in counting, geometry, and measurement.

DOMAIN: Science

Growth and accomplishments	Samile is fascinated with the science area and chooses to go there often. He makes use of the tools provided (magnifying glasses, balance scale) and eagerly joins in various scientific experiments, making observations and asking questions.
We will continue to work on	supporting his interest in science both inside and out!

(continued on next page)

Teachers link the written report directly to the portfolios. By doing so, they are connecting their conclusions to their evidence for those conclusions; therefore, the portfolio items should be shared with children's families right along with the report. The descriptions (and accompanying photos and work samples) on the portfolio forms will make the report come alive for families. They will see their child in action and appreciate how she demonstrates her skills and capabilities.

"The evaluation reports really helped me focus on what I was going to talk about with the families. And the families really felt that parent/ teacher connection because of these formats." —Danielle

"This really helped me to share more with the families when I met with them for IEP meetings. The photos I included have been so powerful. I describe the activity to the child's family members and tell them what their child was doing. It's hard for them to visualize, so the photos and my written descriptions really help." —Cathy

The portfolio documentation and a copy of the evaluation reports should be presented to the family for them to keep. Programs do not have the space to keep the portfolios of all of the children enrolled over the years, but they usually do have the capability to keep a copy of the evaluation reports (even storing them electronically). And families treasure the portfolios! They see them as a keepsake, a wonderful way to remember what their child was doing in his time at the early childhood program. It's important for teachers to honor the interest that families have in this documentation and know that their hard work at collecting the items in the portfolio was well worth it.

Setting Up Meetings with Individual Families

In chapter 2, we began creating the Developmental Study with a conversation with each child's family members. For some this conversation might have taken place as the child was being enrolled in the early childhood program. For others it might have been conducted during a home visit. The Individual Child Information Record was the format on which to gather information about the child from his family members. As time has gone by and other formats were completed for the Developmental Study, the teacher's knowledge about the child has continued to grow. She has learned more about

- who each child is,
- what his interests are, and
- in what domains and learning goals he showed strengths and weaknesses.

Throughout the information-gathering process, teachers should be communicating with families regularly. But daily conversations and e-mails and texts should not be about evaluating the children, whether reporting that they "had a good day" or raising a concern. When teachers want to communicate with families about how their child is doing in the early childhood program, they should set up a face-to-face meeting at a mutually agreed upon time. Most programs do so two or three times across the program year so that teachers can share with families what they are learning about their children.

But what are the purposes of each meeting, and which documentation or evaluation pieces do teachers share? Here are four plans for setting up meetings with individual families. Teachers should discuss the options for family meetings with their administrators and colleagues and determine what plan is best for their program.

Plan 1: Three Meetings across the Program Year (with one summary report)

Timing	Beginning of the year	Late fall	Late spring
Purpose	Get acquainted at an intake meeting and/or a home visit.	Share child's general adjustment to the program and developmental information observed thus far.	Evaluate child's growth and accomplishments and identify what to work on with the child.
Formats shared	Individual Child Information Record	Portfolio documentation (with photos and work samples)	Developmental Study Teacher and Family Reflection Form, portfolio documentation (with photos and work samples), and Family/Teacher Summary Report

Plan 2: Three Meetings across the Program Year (with two summary reports)

Timing	Beginning of the year	Late fall	Late spring
Purpose	Get acquainted at an intake meeting and/or a home visit.	Share child's general adjustment to the program, evaluate the child's growth and accomplishments, and identify what to work on with the child.	Evaluate child's growth and accomplishments and identify what to work on with the child.
Formats shared	Individual Child Information Record	Portfolio documentation (with photos and work samples) and Family/Teacher Summary Report	Developmental Study Teacher and Family Reflection Form, portfolio documentation (with photos and work samples) and Family/Teacher Summary Report

Plan 3: Four Meetings across the Program Year (with one summary report)

Timing	Beginning of the year	Late fall	Late winter	Late spring
Purpose	Get acquainted at an intake meeting and/or a home visit.	Share child's general adjustment to the program and developmental information observed thus far.	Share teacher reflections about the child's interests, strengths, and plans for next steps.	Evaluate child's growth and accomplishments and identify what to work on with the child.
Formats shared	Individual Child Information Record	Portfolio documentation (with photos and work samples)	Developmental Study Teacher Reflection Form	Developmental Study Teacher and Family Reflection Form, portfolio documentation (with photos and work samples), and Family/Teacher Summary Report

Plan 4: Four Meetings across the Program Year (with two summary reports)

Timing	Beginning of the year	Late fall	Late winter	Late spring
Purpose	Get acquainted at an intake meeting and/or a home visit.	Share child's general adjustment to the program, evaluate the child's growth and accomplishments, and identify what to continue to work on with the child.	Share teacher reflections about the child's interests, strengths, and plans for next steps.	Evaluate child's growth and accomplishments, and identify what to work on with the child.
Formats shared	Individual Child Information Record	Portfolio documentation (with photos and work samples) and Family/Teacher Summary Report	Developmental Study Teacher Reflection Form	Developmental Study Teacher and Family Reflection Form, portfolio documentation (with photos and work samples), and Family/Teacher Summary Report

As you can see, the most significant differences in the meeting plans above are when teachers shift to evaluating a child's progress. In plans 1 and 3, they do so only once in the late spring. In plans 2 and 4, they share evaluation information twice—in late fall and in late spring. In the late fall meetings for plans 1 and 3, they share just the portfolio documentation. They are sharing evidence and not shifting to the evaluative mode. They are saying to the child's family members: "Here's what we have seen her do thus far related to developmental standards." For late fall meetings in plans 2 and 4, they add the evaluation piece by completing the Family/Teacher Summary Report. This means they not only present the portfolio evidence, but they identify the child's growth and accomplishments and what to work on next with the child. It's important for teachers to consider how they want to collect information and when they want to move from documentation to evaluation.

Planning for Effective Meetings with Families

No matter how many formal meetings are scheduled, teachers are still ready to arrange meetings with families if they express a need to do so. Family members may initiate a meeting because they are concerned about something their child said happened at school or they want to understand more about the curricular approaches used at the program. Teachers may initiate a meeting because they want to make clear some of the expectations of the program regarding attendance or health. At times these meetings may have to focus on difficult topics such as biting or use of bad language. In these conversations, both teachers and families agree that they are partners working toward the benefit of the child and maintain respectful communication throughout.

Whether the purpose of the meeting is to get acquainted, to review a portfolio, to evaluate the child's progress, or to discuss a difficult topic, there are steps teachers can take to make the family feel comfortable, to set a positive and welcoming tone, and to engage in meaningful and respectful conversation. When teachers engage in ongoing conversations with families at drop-off and pickup times as well as when they see each other out in the community, they have opportunities to build trusting and open relationships. These informal conversations should always be positive. Perhaps the teacher tells a story about the child's interests or new explorations. This is not the time for evaluation or reporting of concerns. Because other families may be nearby, teachers must be very careful to consider confidentiality by only discussing general and positive topics. If more serious issues need to be addressed, teachers find a private space within which to hold a discussion. As the relationships between teachers and families grow and deepen, teachers can plan for more formal meetings with the following in mind:

1   Accommodate family needs in scheduling meetings. Not all families can attend family/teacher conferences in the middle of the workday. It's important that teachers consider flexible scheduling.

2   Set up a pleasant meeting environment (adult-sized chairs placed around a clutter-free table).

> Placing a vase with flowers on a nearby table along with coffee or lemonade and cookies is another way of saying, "I'm glad you're here." (Gronlund and Engel 2001, 222)

3   Communicate with an open, friendly, and supportive attitude. Be sensitive to cultural norms and different ways of communicating.

4   Be clear about the time frame of the meeting and offer to watch the time. This sets expectations and puts family members at ease. If more time is needed for discussion, arrangements can be made for another meeting in person or by phone.

5   Invite family members to talk first and value their thoughts and questions about their child. Such questions might include the following:

   - What does your child like about our program?
   - Is there any information you would like me to know about your child?
   - What do you hope we'll accomplish today? (Gronlund and Engel 2001, 224)

6   Share the documentation that shows what the child is doing at the program. And throughout that sharing, continually invite feedback, comments, and questions from the family.

7   Share evaluative conclusions in positive ways while setting goals to address areas of concern. Teachers refer to their documentation to show the evidence that supports their conclusions, and they invite the families to join them in goal setting for the child.

8   Identify ways for further communication to take place. Teachers may offer e-mail or telephone support to continue the conversation or may need to schedule a follow-up meeting.

9   Thank family members for coming. Many teachers end the conference by telling the family something that delights them about the child. Even after difficult conversations, these kinds of positive comments can go a long way to contribute to a strong partnership with families.

Conclusion

Conducting effective meetings with families can be challenging for teachers. Some families do not feel comfortable in an educational setting. They may feel as though teachers are somehow judging their parenting skills. They may be fearful of what teachers are going to tell them about their child. It's important for teachers to engage in ongoing communication that is warm, friendly, and positive so that a mutual feeling of trust and respect is nurtured with children's family members. Then families and teachers can truly be on the child's team, working together to benefit each child!

In the next chapter, we will look at practical considerations when creating Developmental Studies. Many suggestions will be given to guide teachers in this process.

11 Practical Considerations When Creating Developmental Studies

I set out in this book to recapture the joy educators feel when working with young children, to find delight in their time with them. I encouraged teachers to think about individual children, to relish their differences, to build curriculum around their interests, and to plan for meaningful play experiences for them. I also integrated ways to be accountable to the demands placed on teachers to document children's learning. I gave strategies for making that documentation fit into an early childhood program so that teachers can still be very much in the moment with the children, fully present and engaged with them. I offered many suggestions and formats to help teachers create meaningful documentation that they can use to better plan for each child under their care. I also emphasized the importance of ongoing communication with children's families so that a true, trusting, and reciprocal partnership is formed.

Throughout the book, I have shared comments from teachers who have created Developmental Studies for the children in their programs. Here is more feedback about their experiences.

"Creating the Developmental Studies puts individualization and differentiation in the front of my mind. Completing the pieces of documentation each month helped keep each child's needs fresh." —Sara

"As I started thinking about the children and completing the documentation for the Developmental Studies, I realized that I wanted to know each one better, to connect with each one more fully." —Jordan

"This process caused me to look at the children in a different light. It opened up new avenues for me so that I tweaked my teaching and presented things differently to the children." —Cathy

"This streamlines the whole process. We're able to connect what we know about the child to our planning for next steps. This helps us discuss our children and pull it all together." —Sara

Challenges of Creating Developmental Studies

The model of a Developmental Study shared in this book is one way to consider individualizing curriculum. It is based on documented observations that help teachers identify each child's needs and the planning strategies to address those needs. The formats were designed to provide a step-by-step process that teachers can use as they work with young children over the course of a year, with the goal of creating a full Developmental Study for each child during that time. This can be challenging for teachers. In addressing these challenges, it's important to continually remember the purpose of the process: to individualize curriculum based on documented evidence and to delight in each child! If that delight is being lost, the process is not worthwhile.

To maintain the joy of teaching young children, teachers need to keep two expectations in mind when creating Developmental Studies:

1   To complete as much of the documentation as possible
2   To be flexible and forgiving to themselves in the process

A learning curve is involved any time teachers try something new. Some formats will make more sense or be easier to implement than others. Some might present more challenges and require more time and effort to complete. Talking with colleagues can help immensely. Teachers can share their successes and challenges and exchange ideas for time-efficient strategies for collecting meaningful documentation. Coteachers can work together in a team, dividing up tasks, routinely sharing information with each other (remember our Take Five meeting suggestion?), and encouraging each other's efforts. Reviewing the two examples of completed Developmental Studies in appendix A can help guide teachers in completing their documentation. And remembering to smile and enjoy what you are learning about the children will make the process seem less overwhelming and remind you of the purpose for what you are doing.

"The examples are great, very helpful. We go back and look at them regularly. Sometimes we panic that we're not doing things right, and then we look at the examples and feel better. As coteachers, we can also joke around and focus on the children. It's a more fun conversation, and you end up laughing about things the children did." —Linda

"By taking the time to put our thoughts in order about each child, we definitely come out feeling more energy for each one and are excited about particular plans." —Jarrod

Being Flexible

Sometimes life gets in the way of creating a full set of documentation. Perhaps it's a tough winter and many days of school are canceled due to extreme cold temperatures and snowfall. Or perhaps some of the children's attendance is poor and it's difficult for teachers to observe them as extensively as those who attend consistently. Working with their administrators and teaching colleagues, teachers can determine priorities in gathering documentation and using it effectively to individualize curriculum. Here are more teacher comments related to the challenges of creating Developmental Studies.

"We're just having a really busy year, so it's been challenging to complete the documentation. But when I go through it, I'm glad that I've done it." —Jordan

"We have found we had to adapt the timing of the documentation, which gave us a chance to figure this process out and make it our own." —Linda

"Creating the Developmental Studies has helped us to be more accountable to the students." —Sara

"This process highlights the importance of having systems ensconced in your practice for how you observe, document, and plan. Anyone can do this pretty well with good instincts, but when there's a system in place, the documentation with a specific timetable, it forces us to do the careful thinking that we're capable of doing—it makes us think more about the children. Without a system, we might not do it. It provides accountability. It helps us make sure that we do it well." —Jarrod

Adapting the Process

Teachers can certainly make adaptations to the process to better fit their needs. As they review the aspects of a Developmental Study and consider the ways in which they want to move forward in individualizing curriculum, they can choose the strategies that will make this process successful for them. Here are two ways that teachers have adapted the process:

1   Choosing the formats and pieces of documentation that are most meaningful and appropriate for your program
2   Focusing on a small group of children at a time for this kind of in-depth reflection and planning

Let's look at each of these adaptations more closely.

CHOOSING FORMATS

The documentation formats that make up a complete Developmental Study for each child include the following:

- an Individual Child Information Record
- a Child Interest Survey and/or Choice Record
- an Individualized Play Planning Sheet
- four to seven portfolio forms (for observations in the fall)
- a Developmental Study Teacher Reflection Form
- an Individualized Goal Planning Sheet
- four to seven portfolio forms (for observations in the spring)
- a Developmental Study Teacher and Family Reflection Form
- a Family/Teacher Summary Report

Teachers and administrators in an early childhood program can consider the list above and choose among the formats. The group may decide that they already get the information included on the Individual Child Information Record in their enrollment documents as new families come into their program. Many programs already have ways that they report information to families similar to the Family/Teacher Summary Report. They may use the narrative summary from their authentic assessment tool or one that they designed especially for their program. The staff at an early childhood program can discuss and determine which of the pieces of documentation listed above are redundant and not necessary to include in their Developmental Studies.

Another way to consider the list above is to think in terms of starting slowly and working toward completing full Developmental Studies on the children in the program over a two- to three-year period. Here is one model for that approach.

	Documentation to Complete for Each Child
Year 1	Individual Child Information Record • 2–3 portfolio forms in fall • 2–3 portfolio forms in spring • Developmental Study Teacher and Family Reflection Form
Year 2	All of the above and add: • Child Interest Survey and/or Choice Record • Individualized Play Planning Sheet • Increase to 3–4 portfolio forms in fall • Increase to 3–4 portfolio forms in spring • Add Family/Teacher Summary Report
Year 3	All of the above and add: • Developmental Study Teacher Reflection Form • Individualized Goal Planning Sheet

Each group of teachers and administrators will need to determine which parts of the Developmental Studies are most helpful and meaningful to them. The goal of individualizing curriculum and meeting each child's needs will guide the discussions about how best to implement this process.

FOCUSING ON A SMALL GROUP OF CHILDREN

Another strategy that has been successful for teachers when implementing this approach is to focus on a small group of children. In this way teachers engage in deep reflection and planning for a few children at a time rather than in creating the full set of documentation for every child. They are practicing individualization and are learning more about how best to address children's needs by focusing on a small group.

This strategy works only because the planning process in the Developmental Studies always includes thinking about other children who might benefit. I never want to communicate that some children are more important than others. Rather, I want to make the process of individualizing curriculum one that is doable and not overwhelming for teachers. Sometimes when teachers first approach planning with individual children in mind, they feel as though they must completely change everything they are doing and plan lessons for each of the children in their classroom! This is not the way I am looking at individualized curriculum. Instead, I am asking teachers to consider the following:

- Who is each child as related to his family, life experiences, cultural heritage, developmental strengths, and growing skills?
- What are his interests and choices?
- What other children show the same interests and choices?
- How can a teacher best plan for the groups that show similar interests and choices?
- What are the developmental goals for each child?
- What other children would benefit from plans to address the same developmental goals?
- What are the results of the implemented plans for all of the children?

So even if a teacher creates Developmental Studies for three to six children at a time, she will still be addressing the needs of all of the children in her class. When the staff at an early childhood program decides that focusing on a few children is the best way to begin implementing Developmental Studies, there are some important things to keep in mind.

Teachers need to choose carefully the children on whom to focus. They want to choose a variety of individuals, not children who are all developing in the same ways. They may want to consider including a child who is developing typically for her age, one who is showing greater capabilities and needs to be challenged more than other children, and one who is not quite at age-level in his developmental capabilities. They may look at children's personality traits and choose one child who is more outgoing and another who is more timid. They may ask themselves, "What children are more puzzling to me? Which ones do I want to understand better?" These are important considerations. The more variety in the small group of children on whom they will focus, the more their conclusions can be applied to the whole group. Here are some teacher comments about choosing children on whom to focus.

"My coteacher and I did a really good job selecting different children. Each one has at least one other child in the classroom who is very similar and benefits from the plans we make. We can immediately apply what we're thinking of for one of our focus children and then apply it for other children." —Sara

"The children whom I'm working with aren't necessarily my most challenging children in the class. They're pretty middle or high in their achievement. But this has forced me to stop and look at moments with them. I might reflect, 'Oh, I didn't realize this was a challenge for her.' It's made me kind of pause and not give the middle kids the short end of the stick. It's made me look at these other students and see what they need." —Jordan

Teachers will continue to observe and plan for all of the children. The assumptions underlying the creation of Developmental Studies (whether for a few children or for all of them) include teachers engaging in planning for the whole group and in observing all of the children. The individualized strategies I have suggested throughout the book are to be integrated into group planning. If teachers decide to focus on three to six children, they need to continue with whole group planning and observation as well. Here are some teacher comments about the challenges involved in this integration process.

> "Our lesson planning for the whole class is very busy right now. And I realized that the individualized plans that I made for my focus children were too far outside of my everyday planning for the rest of the class. I didn't weave them into my plans for the group. In the future, I'll try to integrate the group and individual goals more fully." —Jarrod

> "We've worked hard to make sure that every child's day is rooted in their interests and that our curriculum is truly emergent. But that hasn't included what my goals were that I set for my focus children! In reflection, I should probably have tried to weave those goals into opportunities within our day." —Jordan

Teachers will build strong partnerships with *all* of the children's families. Being effective early childhood educators means engaging positively with each child's family. Whether or not teachers are focusing on a child and creating a Developmental Study, they still communicate regularly with all of the families in their program. They invite their input about their child and share information with them about what they have observed their child do and how he is progressing. When teachers create Developmental Studies, they continue to use the assessment tools and family reporting strategies that their program has selected. They conference with each of the children's families to discuss the child's strengths, capabilities, and areas on which they are working. It's important for teachers to communicate with their administrators and colleagues to determine how they will share information with all families even when they are focusing on a few children for the purpose of learning more about individualized curriculum.

Conclusion

The job of teaching young children is demanding. Teachers are asked to be continually thinking on the spot, adjusting to the needs of children, and answering to the calls for accountability. Adding the task of completing the formats in the Developmental Study in order to individualize curriculum may feel to some like an add-on rather than a valuable process. However, it's so easy to miss individual children's needs in the busy activity of an early childhood program. By completing documentation about each child, being accountable for that documentation, and engaging in meaningful reflection about what has been observed to plan appropriately for each child, teachers have the opportunity to elevate their own practice to its highest levels. The completed formats in the Developmental Study show that teachers are professional educators who are truly child-focused and continually learning about children. They are researchers and experts in their field!

In our final chapter we will explore ways to continue to individualize curriculum and find delight in each and every child.

12 Continuing the Journey of Delight

Teachers of young children are engaged in very important work—they are in the human being business!

- They are helping develop the future.
- They are brain developers.
- They are supporting the development of the citizens of tomorrow.
- They are touching children's souls in ways that will affect how children change the world, love someone deeply, and raise their own children.

When teachers delight in each child, they are letting that child know they have faith in her, that she is important, and that her uniqueness is wonderful and something to be celebrated. When they recognize a child's competence and are ready to support the child in areas where she needs help, they are giving her confidence to go forward, to take risks, and to learn new things. She will go on throughout life with the voice of her teacher deep within her head: "You can do it. You are capable. You are special. You are you."

> "Peter is a fun-loving, energetic child. He has excellent verbal skills and appears to gravitate toward activities that are more physical, like riding bikes, running, and jumping."

> "I am really struck by how Elena is identifying her feelings more and helping her friends to understand their feelings. She offers hugs and suggests three deep breaths—she's now the peer counselor in the classroom!"

> "Nolan has become the student that you want to showcase for your principal! He has made so much progress over the three years he's been with me. He's a very active and very smart little boy."

"Rebecca really has lightbulbs going off. She's asking questions. She gives information. She's making lots of connections."

Think about the children in your program. What would you write about each one of them? What delights you about each one?

Child's Name	Things That Delight Me about This Child

Thinking Deeply about Each Child

Continuing the journey of delight also involves thinking deeply about each child. Some children are puzzling and some are challenging. Some are easy to reach and some have been affected by life experiences in a way that makes them difficult to reach. They may be distrustful. They may be hungry and sleepy. They may be fearful. These children desperately need the support of their early childhood educators.

To be child-focused and to individualize, teachers must not only delight in children, but must also reflect about them and ask questions that will lead them to plan effective strategies to support each child.

"I find myself puzzled by this child. He's sweet, smart, talkative, and also melancholy. He holds back. How can I reach him?"

> "He's reserved and just lets other children take things from him. I've been trying to figure out why that is. I'm trying to empower him to stand up for himself. I've been doing a lot of modeling, and it's really working well. He's still a little timid about it but is using words more."

> "She is my neediest student. I really wanted to focus on her because sometimes I don't see if this kind of child is making progress. I want to slow down and really look at her more closely. When I started to observe her, I began to see how many things she really *could* do."

Reflect deeply about the children in your program. What puzzles you? What challenges you? What questions do you have about each child?

Child's Name	The Questions I Have about This Child

Maintaining Commitment and Passion in Your Work

Teachers of young children are dedicated people. They must have high energy, enthusiasm, deep reserves of patience, and incredible flexibility. Every moment that they are with the children they are "on," continually taking in information and making in-the-moment decisions on what to do next for both the group and for individual children. This can be exhausting work! So how do early educators maintain their commitment and passion in their work? And, especially, how do they do so in the face of expectations related to accountability, incorporating early learning standards, addressing kindergarten readiness, and assessing children's progress?

Early childhood professionals must remain true to what we know is right for young children! In the face of outside pressures, teachers of young children must know in their hearts what is best for young children. They must familiarize themselves with the recommendations and research that define best practices. They must be ready to explain to others what teaching young children looks and sounds like. They must connect children's play to learning so that others can see the remarkable skills and application of knowledge that children use in high-level, engaging play. They must be ready to demonstrate how they address early learning standards and kindergarten expectations in ways that are just right for the children.

Teachers must protect the early childhood years and advocate against any initiatives that encourage approaches more suitable for older children. Professionals in early childhood education are part educators and part missionaries. They are called to their work and have an ethical responsibility to do no harm to the children in their care.

Maintaining one's joy and passion in such work means teachers must find ways to be supported themselves. This is not a battle one can fight alone. Teachers need to join with colleagues and work together to continue doing what is right for young children. They need tools to help them in their advocacy. Here are some suggestions for support that teachers can enlist as they implement best practices:

- Start ongoing conversations with other early childhood educators at your program to strategize ways to address the challenges you all face.
- Join professional organizations (such as NAEYC and the local state or city affiliate) and attend professional meetings, workshops, and conferences.
- Look for support online in early education blogs, networks, and publications.
- Familiarize yourself with professional recommendations (as found in Copple and Bredekamp's *Developmentally Appropriate Practice*, 3rd ed., early education journals, books, and teacher magazines).

Take a moment to think about the ways you find support as an early childhood professional and identify some new ways you will seek out to make sure you are not standing alone in advocating for best practices.

I find support for best practices by . . .	I will look for additional support by . . .

Delighting in Children and in Life

To find delight in children and their work with them, teachers need to make sure they have a variety of "delights" in their own lives. They need to take care of their physical health as well as their mental and spiritual health. They need to enjoy their loved ones and relish their time with them. They need to take time for themselves—perhaps by exercising, reading, engaging in crafts, cooking favorite foods, gardening, getting together with friends, seeing movies, reading books, and enjoying music or the outdoors. They need to find ways to nourish their souls, whether that is in a loving relationship, a meaningful friendship, a religious community, or a service project.

Take a moment to think about the delights in your life. How are you taking care of your physical, mental, and spiritual health?

I take care of my physical health by . . .	I take care of my mental health by . . .	I take care of my spiritual health by . . .

Conclusion

Why should teachers of young children be child-focused and individualize curriculum? Why should they delight in each child? Because young children deserve nothing less!

> "Engaging in this process of individualizing curriculum has allowed me to see the big picture, to connect the dots and try to learn about the children more fully. Seeing the children's progress in my documentation gives me hope." —Cathy

Appendix A
Two Examples of Completed Developmental Studies

Developmental Study

Child's Name: __Sana__

Teacher's Name: __Danielle__

Program: __University Heights Pre-K__

Dates for the Completion of the Documentation:
__September 2013 – May 2014__

Individual Child Information Record

Child: **Sana**   Date: **9/4**

Culture	Life Experiences	Family	Learning Style	Developmental Strengths
African-American Muslim	Close family Raise chickens Take family walks Go to the park, block parties, orchestra concerts, cultural activities	Mother and father (married) Brother Rhyon, age 12 Sister Summauuah, age 12 Brother Axharr, age 11 Brother Kadar, age 15 Brother Ameer, age 21	Loves to read books with family, play in the sand, and play restaurant.	Communication Vocabulary Active imagination Social Creative
Interests	Emerging Developmental Areas	Approaches to Learning and Responses to Challenges	Emotional Makeup	Physical Needs and Health Issues
Reading, Barbie, babies, Thomas the Tank Engine, playdough, building, drawing and painting, pretending	She's learning more about rhyming and alphabet letters. She is practicing counting 1–10.	She's a risk taker—not afraid to try something new.	Calm, happy, child Can be serious Social, enjoys playing with others Can be silly!	None—very healthy girl

Child Interest Survey

Something I Want to Get Better At

"Know my letters and my numbers."

Something I Want to Learn More About

"I want to read books like my brothers and sisters."

Something Else I Want to Tell You

"I like my school and my teacher."

A Photo of Me

My name is Sana

My Most Favorite Thing to Do at School

"Play in the kitchen and make a restaurant."

My Favorite Play Area and Activity

"The playdough table, building with blocks."

Something I'm Really Good At

"I'm a good drawer and a good painter."

From *Individualized Child-Focused Curriculum: A Differentiated Approach* by Gaye Gronlund © 2016. Published by Redleaf Press, www.redleafpress.org. This page may be reproduced for individual or classroom use only.

Preschool Choice Record

(may be used to tally one child's choices or a group of children's choices)

Child(ren): __Sana, James, Devon, Christina, Michelle, Sofia, Marissa, Caitlyn, David__   Date: __10/2-12__

Art

Sana: IIII
James:
Devon: I
Christina: III
Michelle:
Sofia: II
Marissa:
Caitlyn:
David: IIIII

Blocks

Sana: I
James: IIIIIi
Devon: IIIII
Christina: III
Michelle: II
Sofia: II
Marissa: I
Caitlyn:
David: II

Dramatic Play

Sana: IIIIIIII
James: III
Devon: IIII
Christina: III
Michelle: II
Sofia: IIIII
Marissa: IIIII
Caitlyn:
David: I

Manipulatives

Playdough
Sana: IIIII
James:
Devon: II
Christina: III
Michelle: II
Sofia: IIIi
Marissa: III
Caitlyn: IIIII
David: II

Science/Math

Sana: III
James: II
Devon: IIIIII
Christina:
Michelle:
Sofia: IIII
Marissa: I
Caitlyn: III
David: IIIII

Music/Movement

Sana:
James:
Devon: II
Christina:
Michelle: III
Sofia:
Marissa:
Caitlyn: IIIII
David: I

Library

Sana: IIII
James: II
Devon: III
Christina: IIIIII
Michelle: IIII
Sofia: II
Marissa:
Caitlyn: III
David: IIIII

Sensory Table

Sana:
James: IIIII
Devon:
Christina: III
Michelle: II
Sofia: IIII
Marissa:
Caitlyn: IIIII
David: II

Writing Center

Sana: IIIIIIII
James: II
Devon: II
Christina: IIIIII
Michelle: II
Sofia: I
Marissa: IIIIII
Caitlyn: III
David: IIII

From *Individualized Child-Focused Curriculum*...

Individualized Play Planning Sheet

Child's Name: __Sana__   Date: __9/25__   Teacher: __Danielle__

Interests, Favorite Play Areas and Activities That Show the Child's Strengths:

Dramatic Play (especially restaurant), Reading, Drawing

Other Children Who Show Similar Interests and Strengths:

Nicole, Melanie, Fernanda, Cody, Roberto

Plans for Play Experiences to Build on the Child's Interests and Strengths:
(What play area, materials, and teacher support strategies will you plan?)

- Expand on restaurant play by identifying what restaurants are familiar to Sana and others, bring in menus from them, discuss what foods to cook, add writing materials and a cash register, discuss various jobs in the restaurant and the role of customer, help children play out scenes more fully and document with photos and dictation.

- Make books available in every area of classroom as well as outdoors. Invite Sana to read favorite books with peers and tell stories in her own words, draw pictures of her favorite parts, and make her own books.

Results of Implementation of Plan:

For this child:
10/8: Restaurant play has taken off with Sana acting as leader in organizing servers, cooks, and customers. She likes to run the cash register the best and counts out money with 1-1 correspondence up to 7 routinely. She loved the photo documentation and showed her parents the display of restaurant play near our cubbies. Lots of looking at and listening to books going on—much comprehension and attention to details of stories.

For the other children:
Nicole, Cody, and Roberto most active in restaurant play. Cody and Nicole write orders in scribble writing with some letters. Fernanda and Melanie joined in reading with Sana and drew pictures of favorite parts, showing their comprehension of the stories read.

Portfolio Collection Form

Child's Name: __Sana__   Date: __9/25__   Observer: __Danielle__

Domain(s): __Physical Well-Being and Motor Development (Small Muscle); Language and Literacy__

Learning goal(s) demonstrated in this documentation: _____

__Coordinates use of hands, fingers, and wrists to manipulate objects and perform tasks__
__requiring precise movements; communicates ideas in full sentences; demonstrates__
__understanding of story structure__

Check off whatever applies to the context of this observation:

☑ child-initiated activity   ☑ done independently   ☐ time spent (1 to 5 minutes)

☐ teacher-initiated activity   ☐ done with adult guidance   ☑ time spent (5 to 15 minutes)

☐ new task for this child   ☐ done with peer(s)

☑ familiar task for this child   ☐ time spent (more than 15 minutes)

Anecdotal note: Describe what you saw the child do and/or heard the child say (attach a photo or work sample if appropriate).

Sana was drawing and painting at the art table, using her right hand in a three-finger grip to hold the paintbrush and the fine-tipped marker. She used larger controlled movements to paint and smaller ones to draw the person. When I asked her to tell me about her picture, she told me, "It's a story. See, that's me. She said, "And, those are flowers," as she pointed to the painted area. "Here's the story: First, we went to the ice cream store. Then, we went to the park and picked flowers. And then we went home. The end."

See photo.

Portfolio Collection Form

Child's Name: __Sana__ Date: __10-17__ Observer: __Danielle__

Domain(s): __Language and Literacy (Reading—Word Recognition; Writing); Fine Motor__

Learning goal(s) demonstrated in this documentation: _____

__With modeling and support, recognize and name some uppercase and lowercase__

__letters; use fine motor skills and writing tools__

Check off whatever applies to the context of this observation:

☐ child-initiated activity   ☐ done independently   ☑ time spent (1 to 5 minutes)

☑ teacher-initiated activity   ☑ done with adult guidance   ☐ time spent (5 to 15 minutes)

☑ new task for this child   ☐ done with peer(s)   ☐ time spent (more than 15 minutes)

☐ familiar task for this child

Anecdotal note: Describe what you saw the child do and/or heard the child say (attach a photo or work sample if appropriate).

Sana created the attached (see photo) with markers using a three- finger grasp, and told me, "This is my name." At this point, she is aware that writing her name involves making marks on a paper. She does not yet have left-to-right movement or letter-like symbols.

She was able to tell me the letters in her name in the correct order: "S-A-N-A". And she identified those letters when I wrote her name on the paper.

Portfolio Collection Form

Child's Name: __Sana__   Date: __10-22__   Observer: __Danielle__

Domain(s): __Cognition (Math); Approaches to Learning__

Learning goal(s) demonstrated in this documentation: _____

__Sort and classify objects by one or more attributes; compare size; demonstrate__

__initiative; solve problems__

Check off whatever applies to the context of this observation:

☑ child-initiated activity   ☑ done independently   ☐ time spent (1 to 5 minutes)

☐ teacher-initiated activity   ☐ done with adult guidance   ☑ time spent (5 to 15 minutes)

☑ new task for this child   ☐ done with peer(s)

☐ familiar task for this child   ☐ time spent (more than 15 minutes)

Anecdotal note: Describe what you saw the child do and/or heard the child say (attach a photo or work sample if appropriate).

Today Sana selected pinecones from our natural materials basket. She lined them up and then paired one river stone with each of the pinecones. She began moving the pinecones around and eventually had a line of pinecones sorted from the tallest to the shortest. Then she did the same with the river rocks.

See photo.

Portfolio Collection Form

Child's Name: **Sana**   Date: **11-20**   Observer: **Danielle**

Domain(s): **Approaches to Learning**

Learning goal(s) demonstrated in this documentation:

Develop, initiate, and carry out simple plans to obtain a goal; use imagination and

creativity to interact with objects and materials

Check off whatever applies to the context of this observation:

☑ child-initiated activity   ☐ done independently   ☐ time spent (1 to 5 minutes)

☐ teacher-initiated activity   ☑ done with adult guidance   ☑ time spent (5 to 15 minutes)

☐ new task for this child   ☐ done with peer(s)

☐ familiar task for this child   ☐ time spent (more than 15 minutes)

Anecdotal note: Describe what you saw the child do and/or heard the child say (attach a photo or work sample if appropriate).

Today was the start of the second week with our restaurant. Sana was a customer and ordered a cupcake. The child serving her told her that they didn't have any cupcakes. I asked Sana if she could make a cupcake with something in the room. She thought for a minute and then walked over to the art center.

She took a cupcake wrapper from the open-ended material basket and got some playdough. She sat and molded the playdough for a moment and then put it in the cupcake wrapper. She walked over to the restaurant table with her completed cupcake, sat down, and pretended to eat it.

See photo.

Developmental Study Teacher Reflection Form

Child's Name: __Sana__   Teacher: __Danielle__   Reflection Date(s): __2/20__

What can and does this child do? What specific skills does s/he have?

- follows daily routines
- follows 2 step directions
- counts 1–10 with 1-1
- identifies some numbers 1–5
- identifies letters in her name when in context
- can identify some letters out of context
- understands that words are made up of letters
- puts on jacket and zips
- is learning to share with other children
- uses a 3-finger grip when writing or drawing

What would the next steps be for this child in his or her development?

- negotiating with peers
- name-writing without a model
- identify more letters independently
- 1-1 correspondence 1–20
- identify numbers 1–20

What are his or her interests and how does s/he show them?

- writing—frequently makes books, is beginning to use symbolic writing, is using a model to write names and friends' names
- loves restaurant play, playdough
- likes to play family, often wants to be the sister, and asks others to be the mom. Loves to pretend to go out to eat.

What will you plan to do with this child to build on his or her strengths and interests and to work on next steps?

- math provocations
- letter identification and production
- model negotiation skills and gradually release responsibility to Sana

What materials, activities, teacher support, peer support, and special resources will you use?

- Counting: friends at circle time, number songs, dice and number games, playdough with numbers, recipes in dramatic play
- Letter identification and production: Roll-a-Dough letters to build self-confidence; identification of friends' names on carpets and on hooks; letters on easel, salt trays, and playdough cookie cutters; morning sign-in
- Negotiation: model, play with puppets, group discussions

Individualized Goal Planning Sheet

Child's Name: __Sana__   Date: __2/21__   Teacher: __Danielle__

Developmental Learning Goals for This Child:

1. Independently write her name and identify letters in name in and out of context.
2. Use simple strategies to negotiate and resolve conflicts.

Other Children Who Would Benefit from These Goals:

1. James, Devon, Christina, Michelle
2. James, Sofia, Marissa, Caitlyn, David

Plans for Experiences to Work toward These Goals with This Child:

(What play area[s], materials, peer groupings, and teacher support strategies will you plan?)

1. Introduce sign-in sheet in small group and make part of daily arrival; encourage all children to sign artwork, writings, etc., with their names the best they can; provide name cards throughout the classroom as models.
2. Play name games at large- and small-group times using name cards—comparing children's names; identifying letters.
3. Provide alphabet cookie cutters at playdough area; letter stencils at art area; alphabet blocks in manipulatives.
4. In large and small group, introduce puppets who have conflicts and have children help them negotiate.
5. Conduct class meetings when conflicts arise and help children walk through negotiating strategies.

Results of Implementation of Plan:

For this child:
1. Sana is accurately identifying the letters in her name and writing all but the S correctly (she makes 3 curves rather than 2); beginning to write her name without a model; frequently makes books and writes many letter-like strings with some letter-sound correspondence.
2. She is now independently telling friends, "I am using this. . . " and asks for a turn when someone has something she wants.

For the other children:
1. James and Devon are writing their names on their own and can name all the letters! Christina writes the C, I, T, and A, and can name the others. Michelle makes large Ms on her papers.
2. James and Sofia are still engaging in arguing without resolution—but overall, the conflicts in the room have really diminished for all of the children.

167

From *Individualized Child-Focused Curriculum: A Differentiated Approach* by Gaye Gronlund © 2016. Published by Redleaf Press, www.redleafpress.org. This page may be reproduced for individual or classroom use only.

Portfolio Collection Form

Child's Name: **Sana**   Date: **3-11**   Observer: **Danielle**

Domain(s):   **Approaches to Learning; Language and Literacy (Writing, Phonics)**

Learning goal(s) demonstrated in this documentation: _____

Develop, initiate, and carry out simple plans to obtain a goal; use imagination and creativity to interact with objects and materials;

use creative and flexible thinking to solve problems; emergent writing skills; letter-sound correspondence; expressive language

Check off whatever applies to the context of this observation:

☑ child-initiated activity   ☑ done independently   ☐ time spent (1 to 5 minutes)

☐ teacher-initiated activity   ☐ done with adult guidance   ☑ time spent (5 to 15 minutes)

☐ new task for this child   ☐ done with peer(s)

☐ familiar task for this child   ☐ time spent (more than 15 minutes)

Anecdotal note: Describe what you saw the child do and/or heard the child say (attach a photo or work sample if appropriate).

Dramatic play is set up as a pizza shop. Sana frequently chooses to be a server and/or the chef at the shop. Today another child visited the restaurant, and Sana came over to take his order.

"Here's the menu. I'll be right back."
"Okay."
"Can I take your order?"
"I want cheese and pepperoni pizza."
"What do you want to drink?"
"Lemonade."

Sana wrote down his order using letter sounds to figure out the first letter of the word and wrote letter strings of various other letters for the rest of the word. She left and came back with a pizza she made using felt circles, tree cookies, stones, and tile dividers.

"Do you want anything else?"

See photo.

Portfolio Collection Form

Child's Name: __Sana__   Date: __3-27__   Observer: __Danielle__

Domain(s): __Approaches to Learning; Social/Emotional Development (Peer Interactions)__

Learning goal(s) demonstrated in this documentation: _____

__Persist when problems arise; with modeling and support, negotiate to resolve social__

__conflicts; use language to communicate__

Check off whatever applies to the context of this observation:

- ☑ child-initiated activity
- ☐ teacher-initiated activity
- ☐ new task for this child
- ☑ familiar task for this child

- ☐ done independently
- ☑ done with adult guidance
- ☑ done with peer(s)

- ☐ time spent (1 to 5 minutes)
- ☑ time spent (5 to 15 minutes)
- ☐ time spent (more than 15 minutes)

Anecdotal note: Describe what you saw the child do and/or heard the child say (attach a photo or work sample if appropriate).

Sana and another child (who has a severe language delay) were building in the block area. The other child asked Sana for help to "hammer blocks together." Sana went over tot he dramatic play area and got a Home Depot apron, a plastic hammer, and a plastic saw. She brought them back over and helped the child put on the apron. She attempted to tie it but was unsuccessful and asked a teacher for help.

She placed two pieces of wood down on the table and handed the hammer to the other child and used the saw to pretend to cut the wood. The other child tried to take the saw from her. At first, she yelled, "No!" Then she moved the saw away and said to the teacher, "He keeps taking it away from me." I suggested that she use her words, and she said, "I'm using this. You can have it when I'm done." The other child used the hammer, and Sana gave him the saw when she was done.

Portfolio Collection Form

Child's Name: **Sana**   Date: **4-2**   Observer: **Danielle**

Domain(s): **Language and Literacy (Reading, Writing); Fine Motor**

Learning goal(s) demonstrated in this documentation:

Demonstrate an understanding of basic conventions of print; orient books correctly for reading and turn pages one at a time; demonstrate understanding that print carries meaning; emergent writing; control of writing tool; letter-sound correspondence

Check off whatever applies to the context of this observation:

☑ child-initiated activity   ☑ done independently   ☐ time spent (1 to 5 minutes)

☐ teacher-initiated activity   ☐ done with adult guidance   ☑ time spent (5 to 15 minutes)

☐ new task for this child   ☐ done with peer(s)

☑ familiar task for this child   ☐ time spent (more than 15 minutes)

Anecdotal note: Describe what you saw the child do and/or heard the child say (attach a photo or work sample if appropriate).

Sana sat down in the art/writing center, announcing, "I'm gonna make a book." She took a premade book (pages stapled together) and a pencil and crayons. She wrote from left to write with letterstrings separated by spaces on each page. She said several of the words out loud to herself and wrote a corresponding letter or two to represent them:

For *mommy* she wrote *M* and *E*

For *baby* she wrote *B*, *B* and *E*

For *daddy* she wrote *D* and *E*

For *pizza* she wrote *P* and *Z*

I asked her if she would read her book to me. She agreed and said: "Once upon a time there was a mommy chicken, a baby chicken, and a daddy chicken. The mommy chicken was mad at the daddy chicken because he forgot to pick up the groceries. Daddy said, 'Take a deep breath and relax. Pizza is on its way!' Everyone was happy, and the pizza came. Hurray!"

Portfolio Collection Form

Child's Name: __Sana__   Date: __4-12__   Observer: __Danielle__

Domain(s): __Cognition (Math); Approaches to Learning__

Learning goal(s) demonstrated in this documentation: _____

Sort and classify objects; replicate patterns; count with one-to-one-correspondence;

show initiative and persistence; expressive language

Check off whatever applies to the context of this observation:

☑ child-initiated activity   ☑ done independently   ☐ time spent (1 to 5 minutes)

☑ teacher-initiated activity   ☑ done with adult guidance   ☐ time spent (5 to 15 minutes)

☐ new task for this child   ☐ done with peer(s)

☑ familiar task for this child   ☑ time spent (more than 15 minutes)

Anecdotal note: Describe what you saw the child do and/or heard the child say (attach a photo or work sample if appropriate).

We introduced patterning to the children this week, and today Sana announced, "I'm going to make a pattern!" She went to the math area and took out the box of buttons and spent more than five minutes creating piles of buttons that were similar (some the same color, some with the same number of holes, some shiny and metallic, some not). I asked her what kind of pattern she was going to make. "Don't worry. I know," she replied. Then, she created the following pattern, describing the buttons as she did so: "Shiny button, red button, shiny button, red button, shiny button, red button. See, I have 1, 2, 3, 4 patterns. But I have 1, 2, 3, 4, 5, 6, 7, 8 buttons!" She touched each button as she counted.

She created several more AB patterns with the buttons and continued the pattern correctly each time.

Developmental Study Teacher and Family Reflection Form

Child's Name: __Sana__   Age: __4.10__   Date: __5-18__   Teacher: __Danielle__

General Summary of the Child's Interests and Delights, Accomplishments, and Progress

Teacher:

Sana has grown up so much in her Pre-K year! She learned many things and has been a wonderful member of our group. She is helpful to other children and has learned to negotiate when problems arise. She has really enjoyed writing and making books and is making connections to letters and sounds. She loves to pretend, especially related to restaurants. She also loves playdough and creates interesting and creative things with that and with art materials.

Sana has shown exceptional progress across the year in all of her development. Please see the Family/Teacher Summary Report and her portfolio items for more specific information about that.

And thank you for all the support you have given to our Pre-K program this year! I have so enjoyed knowing you and teaching Sana! I wish your family all the best as Sana moves forward into kindergarten!

Family Members:

Thank you, Danielle, for all that you have done for Sana this year. We, too, have seen how much she has learned and the progress she has made. We are so proud of our little girl!

Family-Teacher Summary Report

Child's Name: __Sana_____ Date: __5-18_____

Teacher: __Danielle_____ Program: __Pre-K_____

DOMAIN: Language and Literacy Development

Growth and accomplishments	Sana is able to make letter-sound connections. She writes with her right hand, using a 3-finger grip as she writes her name and copies the names of friends and writes stories using many of the letters she knows. She retells and re-enacts familiar stories and enjoys a variety of reading experiences. (See portfolio.)
We will continue to work on	recognizing and producing rhyming words; using pictures to tell a simple story.

DOMAIN: Social and Emotional Development

Growth and accomplishments	Sana recognizes and identifies her own emotions as well as those of her peers. She uses words to express feelings and is beginning to more successfully negotiate when conflicts arise. She is showing more confidence in her abilities.
We will continue to work on	resolving conflicts with peers independently more frequently than needing an adult.

DOMAIN: Approaches toward Learning

Growth and accomplishments	Sana uses creative and flexible thinking to solve problems during play. She creates items that she needs to complete a plan without seeking adult support or permission. She is taking more risks and using prior knowledge to make decisions and solve problems. (See portfolio examples.)
We will continue to work on	continuing to develop persistence and focus in tasks.

(continued on next page)

(continued from previous page)

DOMAIN: Cognition and General Knowledge

Growth and accomplishments	Sana participates in complex pretend play with peers. During play she takes on various roles, negotiates these roles, and participates in creating a plan of action. (See portfolio examples.)
We will continue to work on	explaining why she chose a solution to a problem. Currently, when asked why she did something, she responds, "I don't know." We'll continue to model thinking aloud about solutions and encourage her to do the same.

DOMAIN: Cognition: Math

Growth and accomplishments	Sana counts from 1–14, keeping 1-1 correspondence consistently through 10. She can create simple AB patterns and identifies numbers 1–10.
We will continue to work on	counting to 20 by ones with increasing accuracy, trying more complex patterning, and learning to count on from a specific number.

DOMAIN: Cognition: Social Studies

Growth and accomplishments	Sana cooperates with friends and seems to have a basic understanding of fairness. She helps keep the classroom safe by using her words or getting teachers' help when she needs it. She follows our daily routines and participates in group activities as a contributing member of our classroom community.
We will continue to work on	developing a basic understanding of maps as actual representations of places.

DOMAIN: Cognition: Science

Growth and accomplishments	Sana makes simple observations and shares them verbally or by drawing pictures. She shows interest in the natural and physical worlds and participates in group science experiences.
We will continue to work on	drawing conclusions about what she sees, giving explanations, and developing an understanding that living things change over time.

Developmental Study

Child's Name: ___Thomas___

Teacher's Name: ___Jarrod___

Program: ___Children's Community School___

Dates for the Completion of the Documentation:
___September 2014 – June 2015___

Individual Child Information Record

Child: **Thomas**   Date: **9/14/14**

Culture	Life Experiences	Family	Learning Style	Developmental Strengths
Mixed race family (mom is white, Dad is Chinese) Dad is doctor. Mom is at home.	Will move to Ohio at end of year.	Mom, Dad, baby brother Jason. No other family nearby.	Active, hands-on. Curious, loves to investigate. Long attention for self-chosen activities.	Independent, confident, creative. Can be very helpful. Has a positive attitude. Shows attention and perseverance.
Interests	Emerging Developmental Areas	Approaches to Learning and Responses to Challenges	Emotional Makeup	Physical Needs and Health Issues
Construction Transportation Pretend, dress-up	Connections with other children Conflict resolution Communicating with others	Perseverance with learning-related challenges—he really sticks with things! He detaches himself when social challenges arise.	Calm, confident, independent. Doesn't get upset easily. Doesn't show excitement often.	N/A

176

From Individualized Child-Focused Curriculum

Child Interest Survey

Something I Want to Get Better At

"Working at the Please Touch Museum and drawing and stickers and writing out words."

Something I Want to Learn More About

"Writing with markers on paper."

Something Else I Want to Tell You

"I can jump really high, see?"

A Photo of Me

My name is Thomas

My Most Favorite Thing to Do at School

"I like playing with cars and with Emma."

My Favorite Play Area and Activity

"Playdough! Oh, and dress up, too."

Something I'm Really Good At

"Climbing and shooting down bad guys."

Preschool Choice Record

(may be used to tally one child's choices or a group of children's choices)

Child(ren): __Thomas, Dylan, Natasha, Kylie, Sam, Sofia__   Date: __10/10–11/14__

Art

Thomas: II
Dylan: III
Natasha:
Kylie: II
Sam:
Sofia: IIII

Blocks

Thomas: IIII
Dylan: IIII
Natasha: I
Kylie:
Sam:
Sofia: II

Dramatic Play

Thomas: II
Dylan:
Natasha: III
Kylie: II
Sam: I
Sofia: III

Manipulatives

Thomas: I
Dylan: II
Natasha: II
Kylie: II
Sam: III
Sofia:

Science/Math

Thomas: III
Dylan: II
Natasha: I
Kylie:
Sam: II
Sofia:

Music/Movement

Thomas:
Dylan:
Natasha:
Kylie: I
Sam: I
Sofia:

Library

Thomas: IIII
Dylan: II
Natasha: III
Kylie: III
Sam: I
Sofia: II

Sensory Table

Thomas:
Dylan: II
Natasha: I
Kylie: I
Sam:
Sofia: II

Writing Center

Thomas:
Dylan: I
Natasha: I
Kylie: II
Sam:I
Sofia: II

From Individualized Child-Focused Curriculum

Individualized Play Planning Sheet

Child's Name: __Thomas__   Date: __10/15__   Teacher: __Jarrod__

Interests, Favorite Play Areas and Activities That Show the Child's Strengths:

Books, building a city with blocks, active outdoor, physical play

Other Children Who Show Similar Interests and Strengths:

Dylan, Natasha

Plans for Play Experiences to Build on the Child's Interests and Strengths:
(What play area, materials, and teacher support strategies will you plan?)

- Support small groups of children in building with big blocks together; encourage communication and planning. Introduce architectural blueprints and help them make one for their plan. Then follow through.

- Provide books in block area about construction sites.

- Take big blocks outside and see if more space encourages more creative building.

Results of Implementation of Plan:

For this child:
10/21: Took blocks outdoors today, and Thomas incorporated leaves, acorns, and sticks into buildings in very creative ways. Talked much more with other children and with me about what he was doing.

For the other children:
Natasha asked if we could take photos of their block structure outdoors. She, Dylan, and Thomas posed for several different pictures, and then we went inside and made a display together. Natasha took the lead in telling the group about their structure. Thomas and Dylan stood nearby and chimed in occasionally with their ideas.

179

Portfolio Collection Form

Child's Name: __Thomas__   Date: __10/11__   Observer: __Jarrod__

Domain(s): __Scientific Thinking, Approaches to Learning, Language__

Learning goal(s) demonstrated in this documentation: _____

__Engages in experimentation, uses senses to explore, focuses on a task, shows__

__curiosity, describes experiences to others__

Check off whatever applies to the context of this observation:

- ☐ child-initiated activity
- ☑ teacher-initiated activity
- ☑ new task for this child
- ☐ familiar task for this child

- ☑ done independently
- ☑ done with adult guidance
- ☐ done with peer(s)

- ☐ time spent (1 to 5 minutes)
- ☐ time spent (5 to 15 minutes)
- ☑ time spent (more than 15 minutes)

Anecdotal note: Describe what you saw the child do and/or heard the child say (attach a photo or work sample if appropriate).

We introduced the children to the idea of mixing colors in playdough by offering them powdered tempera paint to mix into freshly made white dough. Thomas has chosen this center twice this week and spent much time engaged in color mixing. He works quietly by himself. When I ask him what he has discovered, he says "The blue and yellow made it green. But now I'm putting purple on it."

See photo.

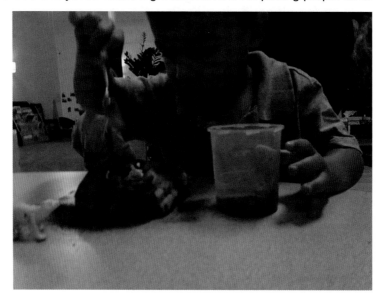

Portfolio Collection Form

Child's Name: **Thomas**   Date: **10/20**   Observer: **Jarrod**

Domain(s): **Fine Motor, Social/Emotional, Approaches to Learning**

Learning goal(s) demonstrated in this documentation:

Demonstrates eye-hand coordination, shows independence, focuses on a task, shows initiative

Check off whatever applies to the context of this observation:

☐ child-initiated activity   ☑ done independently   ☐ time spent (1 to 5 minutes)

☑ teacher-initiated activity   ☑ done with adult guidance   ☑ time spent (5 to 15 minutes)

☑ new task for this child   ☐ done with peer(s)

☐ familiar task for this child   ☐ time spent (more than 15 minutes)

Anecdotal note: Describe what you saw the child do and/or heard the child say (attach a photo or work sample if appropriate).

As part of our fall explorations, children were invited to hammer golf tees into a pumpkin. Once we demonstrated to Thomas how to do so, he did so with ease, carefully aiming the hammer at the head of the golf tee. He chose to do this over the past few days, then, today, announced, "I know what else. I can hammer on the pegboard." He got it off the shelf and again showed eye-hand coordination as he hammered. He worked alone on both activities.

See 2 photos.

Portfolio Collection Form

Child's Name: __Thomas__   Date: __11/2__   Observer: __Jarrod__

Domain(s): __Language and Literacy__

Learning goal(s) demonstrated in this documentation: _____

shows enjoyment of books, understands concepts of print, demonstrates reading

comprehension

Check off whatever applies to the context of this observation:

☑ child-initiated activity   ☑ done independently   ☐ time spent (1 to 5 minutes)

☐ teacher-initiated activity   ☑ done with adult guidance   ☑ time spent (5 to 15 minutes)

☐ new task for this child   ☑ done with peer(s)

☑ familiar task for this child   ☐ time spent (more than 15 minutes)

Anecdotal note: Describe what you saw the child do and/or heard the child say (attach a photo or work sample if appropriate).

Thomas often chooses to go to the class library to look at books. He does so on his own or with friends (Natasha, Kylie, and Dylan). He is familiar with the front, back, and title page, and turns pages carefully as he studies the pictures on each. If he has listened to a teacher read the story before, he often retells it in his own words, demonstrating that he comprehended the key elements of the story. Today he and Dylan looked together at *Pickle Things* and retold the story accurately in their own words, laughing and giggling throughout as they looked at the pictures of "pickle hair" and "pickle trains." Then Thomas came up with his own ideas: "pickle shirt" and "pickle water bottle!"

Portfolio Collection Form

Child's Name: __Thomas__   Date: __11/6__   Observer: __Jarrod__

Domain(s): __Mathematical Understanding, Social/Emotional, Language__

Learning goal(s) demonstrated in this documentation: _____

Geometrical and spatial awareness, mathematical problem-solving, play cooperatively,

communicates with others

Check off whatever applies to the context of this observation:

☑ child-initiated activity   ☐ done independently   ☐ time spent (1 to 5 minutes)

☐ teacher-initiated activity   ☐ done with adult guidance   ☐ time spent (5 to 15 minutes)

☐ new task for this child   ☑ done with peer(s)

☑ familiar task for this child   ☑ time spent (more than 15 minutes)

Anecdotal note: Describe what you saw the child do and/or heard the child say (attach a photo or work sample if appropriate).

Thomas and Dylan frequently build together in the block area. Today they worked for more than twenty minutes to create what Thomas called "tall towers." As they built, they matched similarly shaped blocks. Thomas said, "See, all of these are the same, huh, Dylan? They have to be on the bottom." When blocks fell down, Thomas said, "We gotta build it better so it stands." They each placed the cylindrical pieces carefully to create the towers rising from the foundation. They called to teachers and other children to come and look at what they made.

See photo.

Developmental Study Teacher Reflection Form

Child's Name: __Thomas__   Teacher: __Jarrod__   Reflection Date(s): __2/27__

What can and does this child do? What specific skills does s/he have?

- shows interest and concentration
- has self-help skills
- easily follows daily routines
- expresses ideas and thoughts clearly
- beginning to show more socialization
- plans and solves problems
- showing growing interest in letters (identifying some in his name)
- enjoys listening to and looking at books
- counts but without consistent 1-1
- shows eye-hand coordination but not in writing yet
- shows balance and gross motor coordination

What would the next steps be for this child in his or her development?

- develop 1-1 correspondence in counting
- engage in writing more frequently
- identify more letters independently
- increase social interactions

What are his or her interests and how does s/he show them?

- reading—chooses often, loves funny stories, shares with others
- loves block building and playdough
- likes to be physical and active

What will you plan to do with this child to build on his or her strengths and interests and to work on next steps?

- work more with him on counting, quantities, mathematical understanding
- letter identification in his name, beginning to write his name
- pair him with other children of similar interests to build stronger friendships

What materials, activities, teacher support, peer support, and special resources will you use?

- Provide counting books; counting challenges as he builds with blocks; play counting games
- begin daily sign-in for all children with name cards provided as models; be ready to support Thomas (and others)
- pair with Dylan, Natasha, Kylie, and Sam in different activities

Individualized Goal Planning Sheet

Child's Name: __Thomas__   Date: __2/11__   Teacher: __Jarrod__

Developmental Learning Goals for This Child:

1. Building friendships and socialization
2. Engage in emergent writing

Other Children Who Would Benefit from These Goals:

1. Dylan, Sam, Kylie
2. Kylie, Natasha, Sam

Plans for Experiences to Work toward These Goals with This Child:

(What play area[s], materials, peer groupings, and teacher support strategies will you plan?)

1. Challenge Thomas, Dylan, and Sam to build something together with blocks indoors and out—be nearby to help facilitate social interaction and cooperation.
2. Invite Thomas to "read" to Kylie in the library—share favorite books.
3. Start daily sign-in sheet with name card models for all children. Be ready to support Thomas (and others).
4. Place clipboards around room for children to write on. Model reasons for writing (interviewing friends, labeling creations, writing letters to each other).

Results of Implementation of Plan:

For this child:
1. Thomas has definitely increased in social interactions and cooperative play. He is even acting as leader in planning for dramatic play and block-building scenarios.
2. Thomas is writing the *T, o, m,* and *s* of his name consistently at sign-in and on drawings and paintings.

For the other children:
1. Sam is not as involved in cooperative play, yet. Dylan and Thomas often engage with each other, problem solve, and talk.
2. Kylie loves reading with Thomas, and both are making sense of familiar print through the pictures and repeated listening.
3. Natasha and Sam write their names independently. Kylie is beginning to make recognizable *K*s.

Portfolio Collection Form

Child's Name: __Thomas__   Date: __3/8__   Observer: __Jarrod__

Domain(s): ___Mathematical Understanding, Social/Emotional, Language, Approaches to Learning___

Learning goal(s) demonstrated in this documentation: _____

Geometrical and spatial awareness; mathematical problem-solving; counting with one-to-one correspondence; play cooperatively; communicates with others; persistence

Check off whatever applies to the context of this observation:

- ☑ child-initiated activity
- ☐ teacher-initiated activity
- ☐ new task for this child
- ☑ familiar task for this child

- ☐ done independently
- ☐ done with adult guidance
- ☑ done with peer(s)

- ☐ time spent (1 to 5 minutes)
- ☐ time spent (5 to 15 minutes)
- ☑ time spent (more than 15 minutes)

Anecdotal note: Describe what you saw the child do and/or heard the child say (attach a photo or work sample if appropriate).

Thomas, Dylan, Kylie, and Sam have been working with the Magna-Tiles over the past few days, trying to figure out how high they could build them without them falling down. Thomas has taken the lead with the group and tried to engage them in planning before building. Although he doesn't always get cooperation with that, he helps the group problem-solve strategies for holding on to the structure at various points as it gets taller and taller. If it falls, he shows no frustration. Rather, he says, "Okay, guys, let's do it again!"

See photo.

Portfolio Collection Form

Child's Name: __Thomas__   Date: __3/14__   Observer: __Jarrod__

Domain(s): __Scientific Thinking, Approaches to Learning, Language__

Learning goal(s) demonstrated in this documentation: _____

__Uses senses to explore, shows curiosity, engages in give-and-take conversations__

_____

Check off whatever applies to the context of this observation:

☐ child-initiated activity   ☐ done independently   ☐ time spent (1 to 5 minutes)

☑ teacher-initiated activity   ☑ done with adult guidance   ☑ time spent (5 to 15 minutes)

☑ new task for this child   ☐ done with peer(s)

☐ familiar task for this child   ☐ time spent (more than 15 minutes)

Anecdotal note: Describe what you saw the child do and/or heard the child say (attach a photo or work sample if appropriate).

We made lasagna noodles from scratch as part of our construction unit (constructing lasagna!). Thomas helped measure the flour, salt, and water to make the dough. He followed the directions given and talked with the teacher and others about the changes he observed. As the water mixed with the flour, he said, "Look! It's getting wet and sticky." He was invited to stir the dough and said, "There's big lumps in there. That won't make good lasagna." When he saw how the pasta maker rolled the dough into noodles, his eyes got wide. "Oh, it mushes it so the noodles are smooth and skinny."

See photo.

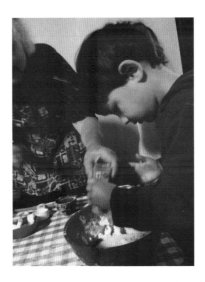

Portfolio Collection Form

Child's Name: __Thomas__   Date: __3/18__   Observer: __Jarrod__

Domain(s): __Fine Motor, Social/Emotional, Approaches to Learning__

Learning goal(s) demonstrated in this documentation: _____

__demonstrates eye-hand coordination, plays and works cooperatively, focuses on a__

__task, shows persistence__

Check off whatever applies to the context of this observation:

☑ child-initiated activity   ☐ done independently   ☐ time spent (1 to 5 minutes)

☐ teacher-initiated activity   ☐ done with adult guidance ☑ time spent (5 to 15 minutes)

☐ new task for this child   ☑ done with peer(s)

☑ familiar task for this child   ☐ time spent (more than 15 minutes)

Anecdotal note: Describe what you saw the child do and/or heard the child say (attach a photo or work sample if appropriate).

Thomas has shown more interest in puzzles and often chooses more challenging and trickier ones. Today he and Sam worked together with the gears, attempting to put them together so that they connected and rotated correctly. They had to reposition them several times, discussing which ways to place them and experimenting with trial and error. As they worked, Thomas began to chant, "We're not giving up! We're not giving up!" and Sam and even other children in the area joined in. I made one suggestion regarding the placement of a gear. Thomas repositioned it, and he and Sam cheered as the gears turned successfully.

Portfolio Collection Form

Child's Name: __Thomas__   Date: __4/2__   Observer: __Jarrod__

Domain(s): __Language and Literacy__

Learning goal(s) demonstrated in this documentation: _____

shows enjoyment of books, understands concepts of print, demonstrates reading

comprehension

Check off whatever applies to the context of this observation:

☑ child-initiated activity   ☐ done independently   ☐ time spent (1 to 5 minutes)

☑ teacher-initiated activity   ☑ done with adult guidance   ☑ time spent (5 to 15 minutes)

☐ new task for this child   ☑ done with peer(s)

☑ familiar task for this child   ☐ time spent (more than 15 minutes)

Anecdotal note: Describe what you saw the child do and/or heard the child say (attach a photo or work sample if appropriate).

Thomas continues to show great interest in books. He looks at them, acts them out, and listens to them when read aloud by a teacher. Today he invited other children to listen to him read to them from the big books we keep in the class library. He read *Jump, Frog, Jump* and *The Little Gingerbread Man* by turning the pages, studying the pictures, and retelling in his own words (but with obvious comprehension of the story lines that he has heard read aloud).

See photo of him enjoying a group reading experience.

Developmental Study Teacher and Family Reflection Form

Child's Name: __Thomas__   Age: __4.2__   Date: __6-8__   Teacher: __Jarrod__

General Summary of the Child's Interests and Delights, Accomplishments, and Progress

Teacher:

Thomas has seemed to enjoy everything we do at school and relish each opportunity. He seems well prepared to confidently and flexibly negotiate your planned transition with your move to Ohio and a new school for him next year.

It has been a pleasure having Thomas in the Oaks Class for the past two years. We wish him and your whole family much joy on the journey ahead!

Family Members:

Our family will miss Children's Community School so much! Thank you for giving Thomas such a strong start in his education. We can see that he has learned so much.

Family-Teacher Summary Report

Child's Name: __Thomas__   Date: __6-8__

Teacher: __Jarrod__   Program: __Oaks Classroom, Children's Community School__

DOMAIN: **Language and Literacy Development**

Growth and accomplishments	Thomas loves looking at and listening to books and sharing them with others. He shows excellent reading comprehension and is beginning to make some letter/sound connections and identify letters correctly. He shows some interest in writing and makes some of the letters of his name correctly. (See portfolio.)
We will continue to work on	engaging in emergent writing more frequently, identifying more letters and sounds.

DOMAIN: **Social and Emotional Development**

Growth and accomplishments	Thomas shows confidence in himself and excitement about learning. He has really increased his socialization this year, making friendships, engaging in more cooperative play, and leading the group in planning and problem-solving. (See portfolio.)
We will continue to work on	resolving conflicts with peers through talking rather than withdrawing from the situation, expressing feelings verbally.

DOMAIN: **Approaches toward Learning**

Growth and accomplishments	Thomas demonstrates persistence and focus even when problems present themselves. He takes initiative and shows independence routinely. (See portfolio.)
We will continue to work on	supporting his strengths in this domain.

(continued on next page)

(continued from previous page)

DOMAIN: Cognition and General Knowledge

Growth and accomplishments	While Thomas willingly participates in our planned curriculum, his primary interests are the elaborate projects and games that he invents (i.e., building complex structures, sailing pirate ships, or organizing bike races). He is a planner, an organizer, and a communicator of his ideas and understanding.
We will continue to work on	balancing his interests with other activities within the classroom that will expand his general knowledge and allow him to apply his deep thinking skills.

DOMAIN: Mathematical Understanding

Growth and accomplishments	Thomas uses deep sense of geometry and spatial awareness in construction with blocks. He's beginning to understand counting with 1-1 correspondence with our support. He engages in mathematical problem-solving that shows he understands more and less. (See portfolio.)
We will continue to work on	counting with greater confidence and accuracy.

DOMAIN: Science

Growth and accomplishments	Thomas engages in sensory and scientific explorations with interest and curiosity. He loved our space exploration unit and developed an extensive and accurate vocabulary regarding the various topics explored. (See portfolio.)
We will continue to work on	making predictions about results of investigations, exploring the natural and physical worlds.

DOMAIN:

Growth and accomplishments	
We will continue to work on	

Appendix B
Formats and Frameworks

Developmental Study

Child's Name: _____

Teacher's Name: _____

Program: _____

Dates for the Completion of the Documentation:

_____

Preschool Weekly Planning and Reflection Framework

DATE:		MONDAY	TUESDAY	WEDNESDAY	THURSDAY	FRIDAY
Large group	Learning goal					
	Activity and teacher strategy					
Small group	Learning goal					
	Activity and teacher strategy					

Plans for Building Community and Relationships	Plans for Outdoor Explorations	Plans for Meals and Transitions

197

Preschool Weekly Planning and Reflection Framework

OBSERVATIONS, MODIFICATIONS, AND REFLECTIONS

MODIFICATIONS FOR INDIVIDUAL CHILDREN:

FOCUSED OBSERVATIONS:

PLANS: Based on your reflections, what will you change for next week?

REFLECTIONS: What worked? What didn't? What did you learn about individual children and group interests?

Individualized Play Planning Sheet

Child's Name: _____ Date: _____ Teacher: _____

Interests, Favorite Play Areas and Activities That Show the Child's Strengths:	Other Children Who Show Similar Interests and Strengths:
Plans for Play Experiences to Build on the Child's Interests and Strengths: (What play area, materials, and teacher support strategies will you plan?)	
Results of Implementation of Plan:	

Quick Check Recording Sheet

Children's Names	Date and Activity	Date and Activity	Date and Activity	Date and Activity

Brief Notes Recording Sheet

Children's Names	Date and Activity

Small-Group Observation Form

Date _____   Activity: _____

Goal(s): _____

Child's Name:	Child's Name:	Child's Name:
Child's Name:	Child's Name:	Child's Name:
Child's Name:	Child's Name:	Child's Name:
Child's Name:	Child's Name:	Child's Name:

Individual Adjustments

For week of: _____   Teacher: _____

Child's Name	Planned Adjustment	Child's Name	Planned Adjustment

Developmental Study Teacher and Family Reflection Form

Child's Name: _____ Age: _____ Date: _____ Teacher: _____

General Summary of the Child's Interests and Delights, Accomplishments, and Progress

Teacher:

Family Members:

References

Brown, Stuart. 2009. *Play: How It Shapes the Brain, Opens the Imagination, and Invigorates the Soul*. New York: Penguin.

Colker, Laura J. 2015. "Supporting One and All in the Discovering Science Center." *Teaching Young Children/Preschool* 8 (3): 16–17.

Conn-Powers, Michael. 2006. "All Children Ready for School: Approaches to Learning." The Early Childhood Briefing Paper Series. Bloomington, IN: Indiana Institute on Disability and Community.

Copple, Carol, and Sue Bredekamp, eds. 2009. *Developmentally Appropriate Practice in Early Childhood Programs Serving Children from Birth through Age 8*. 3rd ed. Washington DC: National Association for the Education of Young Children.

Curtis, Deb, and Margie Carter. 2011. *Reflecting Children's Lives: A Handbook for Planning Your Child-Centered Curriculum*. 2nd ed. St. Paul, MN: Redleaf Press.

Epstein, Ann S. 2007. *The Intentional Teacher: Choosing the Best Strategies for Young Children's Learning*. Washington, DC: National Association for the Education of Young Children.

Erdman, Sarah, and Meredith Downing. 2015. "The Science of Superheroes." *Teaching Young Children/Preschool* 8 (3): 24–27.

Ginsburg, Kenneth R. 2007. "The Importance of Play in Promoting Healthy Child Development and Maintaining Strong Parent-Child Bonds." *Pediatrics* 119 (1): 182–91. doi:10.1542/peds.2006-2697.

Gronlund, Gaye. 2010. *Developmentally Appropriate Play: Guiding Young Children to a Higher Level*. St. Paul, MN: Redleaf Press.

———. 2013. *Planning for Play, Observation, and Learning in Preschool and Kindergarten*. St. Paul, MN: Redleaf Press.

Gronlund, Gaye, and Bev Engel. 2001. *Focused Portfolios: A Complete Assessment for the Young Child*. St. Paul, MN: Redleaf Press.

Gronlund, Gaye, and Marlyn James. 2013. *Focused Observations: How to Observe Children for Assessment and Curricular Planning*. 2nd ed. St. Paul, MN: Redleaf Press.

Gronlund, Gaye, and Kathy Stewart. 2013. "Intentionality in Action: A Strategy That Benefits Preschoolers and Teachers." In *Developmentally Appropriate Practice: Focus on Preschoolers*. Carol Copple, Sue Bredekamp, Derry Koralek, and Kathy Charner, eds., 113–20. Washington, DC: National Association for the Education of Young Children.

Hirsh-Pasek, Kathy, and Roberta Michnick Golinkoff. 2014. "Playful Learning: Where a Rich Curriculum Meets a Playful Pedagogy." *Preschool Matters . . . Today!* (blog). March 6, 2014. http://preschoolmatters.org/2014/03/06/playful-learning-where-a-rich-curriculum-meets-a-playful-pedagogy/.

Kantor, Rebecca, and Kimberlee L. Whaley. 1998. "Existing Frameworks and New Ideas from Our Reggio Emilia Experience: Learning at a Lab School with 2- to 4-Year-Old Children." In *The Hundred Languages of Children: The Reggio Emilia Approach: Advanced Reflections*. 2nd ed. Carolyn Edwards, Lella Gandini, and George Forman, eds., 313–34. Greenwich, CT: Ablex Publishing.

McClelland, Megan M., and Shauna L. Tominey. 2014. "The Development of Self-Regulation and Executive Function in Young Children." *Zero to Three Journal* 35 (2): 2–8.

Miller, Edward, and Joan Almon. 2009. *Crisis in the Kindergarten: Why Children Need to Play in School*. College Park, MD: Alliance for Childhood.

National Educational Goals Panel. 1995. "1995 National Education Goals Report." http://govinfo.library.unt.edu/negp/reports/goalsv1.pdf.

Perry, Bruce D. 2001. "Curiosity: The Fuel of Development." http://teacher.scholastic.com/professional/bruceperry/curiosity.htm.

RAND Corporation. 2005. "Proven Benefits of Early Childhood Interventions." Edited by Lynn A. Karoly, M. Rebecca Killburn, and Jill S. Cannon. Rand Corporation Research Brief Series. Santa Monica, CA: RAND.

Index

Individualized Goal Planning Sheet

Child's Name: _____ Date: _____ Teacher: _____

Developmental Learning Goals for This Child:

1.

2.

Other Children Who Would Benefit from These Goals:

1.

2.

Plans for Experiences to Work toward These Goals with This Child:

(What play area[s], materials, peer groupings, and teacher support strategies will you plan?)

Results of Implementation of Plan:

For this child:

For the other children:

Developmental Study Teacher Reflection Form

Child's Name: Caleb   Teacher: Isabella   Reflection Date(s): 11/20/19

What can and does this child do? What specific skills does s/he have?

Caleb excels at following directions in all aspects of the classroom. He can trace letters and recognize individual letters in different settings. Caleb can communicate his wants/needs in multiple settings. Caleb can hold a pencil, paintbrush and scissors with the appropriate grasp. With gross motor, Caleb can jump on 1 foot, balance on (both feet, separately), and can climb vertically. Caleb can count to 10 without help and can communicate 1-on-1 correspondence.

What would the next steps be for this child in his or her development?

Two things going forward I would work on are Caleb's communication with peers, overall. As well as writing. I would ~~encourage~~ encourage Caleb to tell me his thoughts and then help him think of meaningful ways to explain that to his peers. For writing, Caleb needs more 1-on-1 time with letter practice.

What are his or her interests and how does s/he show them?

Caleb loves building with blocks, painting and talking about his family. He shows this interest by choosing these activities for choice time.

What will you plan to do with this child to build on his or her strengths and interests and to work on next steps?

Integrating painting into writing would be great for Caleb. Either by having him paint something and write his title/name on it or write a sentence then paint the story. Encouraging him to engage with his peers in choice time would also be beneficial.

What materials, activities, teacher support, peer support, and special resources will you use?

I will definitely use blocks and paint activities to spark interest in growth in these areas. ~~Mmm~~ Caleb will also need both teacher and peer support in order to show improvement.